WRITE THAT ESSAY!

A+

D1607136

To all my students who needed help with their essays:
your questions inspired this book.

I dedicate it to you.

WRITE THAT ESSAY!

A+

A Practical Guide to
Writing Better Essays and
Achieving Higher Grades

Dr Ian Hunter Ph.D.

HUNTER
EST 2010
PUBLISHING

This edition published in 2012 by Hunter Publishing
Originally published in 2008 by McGraw-Hill

Printed in Singapore by Craft Print International

Hunter Publishing, PO Box 24687, Royal Oak, Auckland 1345, New Zealand
For trade sales and distribution enquiries contact: sales@hunterpublishing.co.nz

ISBN: 978-1927181-03-4

A catalogue record for this book is available from the
National Library of New Zealand.

www.writethatessay.org

About the author:

Dr Ian Hunter has more than 20 years' experience in education, having been a lecturer and examiner at universities in New Zealand and the UK. A best-selling author, Ian writes on creativity, innovation, history, education, and business. He lives in Auckland, New Zealand, with his wife Debra and their five children.

CONTENTS

CHAPTER ONE
Introduction   **8**
First Things First   9
The Academic Essay   10
Academic Writing: A Style In Itself   10
Parts Of An Essay—The Basics   12

CHAPTER TWO
The Plan   **13**
Plan To Plan   13
Content   14
Logic   14
Structure   15
Coverage   15
A Simple Method For Planning Your Essay   16

CHAPTER THREE
Getting Down To Business   **20**
The Essay   20
The Introduction   21
On The Question Of 'I'   21
Writing Your Introduction   22
Optional Paragraph For Longer Essays   27
The Body Of The Essay   28
Two Absolutely Vital Things To Remember   33
The Final Sentence   34
Don't Forget Linking Sentences   34
The Conclusion   36

CHAPTER FOUR
The Sentence: Exposed And Explained   **40**
Leave The Simple Sentence Behind   40

The Very Short Sentence   42
Repeating Pattern   42
Adverb At The Front   43
The Em Dash   43
The 'W' Start   44
The Paired-Double   44
Prepositional Phrase   45
Verb At The Start   46
Alliteration   47
Metaphor And Simile   47
Colon: And Flow   47
Good Ol' Red, White, And Blue   48
Acceptable Sentence Length   48

CHAPTER FIVE
A Question Of Structure   **50**
Structure And Length   51
Deciphering Questions   52
Pure Description   52
The Double-Whammy   53
The Think Critical   54
The Quote   55
Writing Qualifying Sentences   56
The Question As A Motif   58
How Many Points To Cover?   59

CHAPTER SIX
Style And You   **60**
The Role Of Opinion   60
The Side Of The Argument That You Take   62
It's All About Perspective   62
Forming Your Opinion   67
On Reading   68
How To Use Quotes   71
The One Idea   73

CHAPTER SEVEN
Referencing And Other Chores   75
Two Types Of Referencing   76
Author/Date   76
Creating A Reference List Using Author/Date   80
Referencing Books And Other Sources Using
  Author/Date System   82
Footnote/Endnote System   86
Referencing: Don't Forget Why   90

CHAPTER EIGHT
Essay Writing For Exams   92
Differences And Similarities Between Exam Essays
  And Course Essays   93
Quick Plans   93
Lightning Introductions   94
How Much Should You Write?   95
Detail And General   96
Using Sub-Headings   97
Using Space To Your Advantage   98
Diagrams   99
The List Of Do-Nots   100
Handwriting   100
Effective Exam Practice   101
Planning Your Time   102

CHAPTER NINE
Polishing Your Work   104
Writing Is Not A Flash Of Brilliance   104
Removing Clever Work   106
Distance And Time   107
Listen To Improve   109
The Trap Of Overwriting   109

Conclusion   111

CHAPTER ONE

Introduction

Whether you are at high school, university, or returning to study after many years—writing essays is one of those tasks in life that many people find difficult. You are unsure how to go about it; you don't know what is expected of you; no one tells you why one essay scores highly and another does not. It does not need to be this way. With a little knowledge and some practice you can write better essays and see your grades improve. More importantly, your confidence will increase, because for the first time you will clearly know how to go about writing an essay and what your marker expects.

In this book I will show you:

- how to plan essays
- how to write great introductions
- what markers are looking for in the body of your essay
- how to make a convincing argument
- which facts to include; which to leave out
- what should be in a conclusion
- how to make your writing more interesting
- different ways of structuring your essays
- how to reference your essays
- how to write essays under exam conditions
- how to polish your sentences

... and many other essay-writing techniques

In short, we will cover essay writing from the inside out. You will learn what few teachers ever teach you in school or university: the craft of essay writing. This is vitally important—not just because you will learn how to express your ideas and thoughts, but because an experienced essay marker can tell within three sentences of your introduction whether or not you know what you are doing. Do you? After reading this book and putting these suggestions into practice, when the marker reads your work, they should be nothing but impressed.

All the suggestions and principles presented in this book have been road-tested on my students over the past 20 years. Hundreds of them struggled to put a few words down on paper, or sat awkwardly for hours waiting for inspiration to strike. It never did. Then, after learning the techniques and methods of writing an essay, they were able to put these ideas into practice and have become fluent and productive writers. Many saw their grades quickly increase 30, 40, 50 per cent or more. You, too, can achieve this kind of success. If you apply the suggestions in this book you will write a better essay. It will require practice and application, but it is well within your grasp.

This book is suited to people at any level of study. These principles have been used with high school students and their essays have improved dramatically; equally, these principles have been explained to 40-year-olds returning to university after a long period away from formal study who are trying to write a master's thesis. Both have benefited. Naturally gifted students have discovered new skills and raised their performance; so, too, have students braving learning difficulties, such as dyslexia. It does not matter which group you fit into, you will find this a helpful book.

First Things First

The first thing to realise is that essay writing is very different from other sorts of writing. It is not like writing a speech or a letter, a business report or a novel, all of which have accepted styles and approaches. Business reports, for example, have a predictable order and specific sections—from the executive summary at the start, to the conclusion and recommendations at the end. So, too, the novel, with its deep characterisation, plot, sub-plots, and climax—all of which must be mastered if you are going to have a shot at becoming the next Jane Austen or Ernest Hemingway. Essay writing is the same, in that you must learn the conventions if you are going to master this form of expression.

The Academic Essay

Academic essays are everywhere. If you have to write an essay on a topic in English, history, geography, economics, business, art, or music, then you will be writing an academic essay. It is called 'academic' purely because it is written to expand on a particular problem or point in a scholarly and informed way. If you see words in your questions like 'examine', 'discuss', 'analyse', 'justify', 'support', or 'investigate'—then you will write an academic essay. Writing this kind of essay does not rely on your creative talent with words but your ability to form a case and put forward an argument.

It does not matter if your essay subject is Ancient Rome, international relations, investment banking, foreign exchange, medieval thought, art in the seventeenth century, continental drift, or the life and times of Charles Dickens. What each of these topics has in common is that the marker will be expecting you to show two things: first, your understanding of the topic; second, your ability to state an argument for a particular point of view. This is always the case. Any question demands a response. In an essay, your response to the question must contain both information and justification. You will need to learn how to say *what* you know and *why* you think your answer is correct.

Just think of yourself having to convince someone on paper why your answer is the best one: that you have the right information and correct solution to the problem that they have posed. This is academic writing. And it does not matter whether you are a high school student or someone coming back to study after many years out of college—if you have to write an essay of this sort, then you are writing an academic essay.

> *Think of yourself having to convince someone on paper why your answer is the best—with each point you make supported by evidence.*

Academic Writing: A Style In Itself

One of the first things to realise is that academic writing is a style in itself. It is not fiction and it is not newspaper writing. These are two of the most common mistakes that are made. As if writing a great novel, the novice essay writer believes that the clincher—their final and most convincing point—should be saved until their brilliant climactic finish. This is wrong. You are writing an academic essay—it is not a detective story and is not structured like one. In an academic essay you make your argument clear from the outset. There should be nothing left unsaid by the end of the first paragraph about your intent and your purpose in the essay. If you are taking a particular point of view—and you should be—you state it up front and in that very first paragraph.

It is then over to you in the rest of the essay to make your case watertight and give substance to the claim that you made at the outset. This is the accepted practice. An experienced marker can usually tell by the end of the first paragraph if the essay will be a top-class piece of work or not, merely because the student has made their argument plain. Someone who knows what is expected of them in writing essays will always do this; someone who has not yet mastered the craft will not. If the latter is you, then do not worry—by the end of this book you will no longer make this mistake.

State your position from the outset. You are not writing a detective story. Leave the reader in no doubt about your argument from the very first paragraph.

Academic writing is not journalism either, and colourful or lazy language will not be rewarded. You do not need lots of vivid adjectives in academic writing. It requires your thought, analytical abilities, precision, and investigative talents: it requires little of your literary creativity or artistic brilliance. There are few prizes for gripping introductions or clever turns of phrase in academic writing. Instead, you will gain your greatest satisfaction from an argument carried soundly, a train of thought logically structured, a paragraph stated well and carefully supported by evidence. These things will become your stock in trade.

In academic writing you must avoid figures of speech such as idioms

and colloquialisms. Do not use common turns of phrase or puffery.
All these will suggest to your marker that you have not yet attained a
competency in academic writing. Your job is to show him or her that
you have. So write clearly, carefully, and convincingly. Now we will
consider how.

Parts Of An Essay—The Basics

An academic essay has three parts: introduction, body, and conclusion.
Each of these parts fulfils a specific role, and a marker will be looking for
your mastery, not only of the material that you are discussing, but also of
the style and structure of academic prose. There is a formula you can
learn and follow. It is easily grasped and once you learn it some of the
difficulties that you presently face in scholarship will disappear.

Of course, some people will say that
I am simplifying things too much. I do
not think so. Like most activities in life, it
is important to master the fundamentals
before attempting more daring challenges.
To think that you could manoeuvre a
Formula One car at high speed would
be foolish if you had not first mastered a
slower variant. Here, with essay writing,
we do the same. We master the basic
style and structure before we try more
innovative approaches.

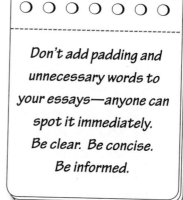

Don't add padding and
unnecessary words to
your essays—anyone can
spot it immediately.
Be clear. Be concise.
Be informed.

Even once you begin to flex your muscles as an essay writer, you
will soon realise that hidden in some of the cleverest writing are the
fundamentals. They might not be there in glaring technicolour; but they
are still on the page. In summary, don't try more daring manoeuvres
with your pen until you have learned what is, and what is not, required
in an academic essay. *Write That Essay!* begins with the fundamentals.
The place we start: the plan.

CHAPTER TWO

The Plan

Plan To Plan

Of all the things people do in essay writing, planning is the one they do the least well. It is so easy to overlook. You feel a surge of creative inspiration—some problem you have been chewing over for several days becomes clear—and immediately you pull out a sheet of paper and begin writing, or jump on the computer and commence typing frantically. What is the problem with this? Well, what normally happens is that all goes well for about ten minutes; or if you are really in the flow, perhaps half an hour. Sentence after sentence flows gracefully from your pen; the screen in front of you is crammed with text. You are impressed. But then, without warning, you turn a corner in your argument and mid-sentence nothing happens. Your inspiration has dried up. Those miraculous creative juices evaporate before your eyes and all you are left with is that sinking question: What am I going to write next?

In a bid to regain your flow, you hastily re-read the previous two or three paragraphs. A few lines in and you begin to frown. Something is wrong. The words that sounded so profound in your head do not read so well in the cold hard light of day. The sentences are disconnected, the points unsupported,

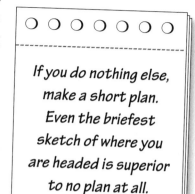

If you do nothing else, make a short plan. Even the briefest sketch of where you are headed is superior to no plan at all.

and the grammar—well, that's another story.

Why is this? You neglected to plan. Most people do. However, if you plan your essay you will not have this kind of experience. Planning gives you four benefits: you get content, logic, structure, and coverage. These four elements do not happen by chance. They take work and thought. Here is where the plan comes in. Even if you think time spent planing is wasted because you are not doing any writing, I will let you in on an examiner's secret—in easily 80 per cent or more of cases a major difference between an A-grade essay and one of a lower grade is the plan.

People who plan their essays write to a logical flow. If you start just any old place and hope to end up somewhere better, you won't. It will be some place a whole lot worse! Do yourself a favour: Plan! Even if you are unsure about the strength of your content, or your argument, the mere fact that you plan your essay and write it to a clear and logical structure will raise your mark.

That's right: if you put two essays together with similar content but one was planned and the other not, the one that was planned will score more highly. Why? Because an obvious structure demonstrates that thought has gone into *what* was said and *how* it was said. Both are important—as the person who plans realises.

Let's look briefly at those four elements of a plan before we go on to consider an easy approach to planning your essay.

Content

Any method of planning an essay must allow you to sketch out your content. This is what the essay is about: the facts, figures, examples, and information. In a plan you don't write this down in detail, but you will refer to it to make sure that you understand the topic and have all the elements that you need.

Logic

Do your thoughts progress naturally from one to the next in an ordered fashion? Will somebody else who is reading your essay be able to follow your train of thought? Logic is about sequence—getting your ideas in the right order; it is also about support—having the correct information to support the point that you have just made. A good planning system will allow you to think about each of these points and avoid making the mistake of having the right ideas but putting them down in a confusing or illogical order.

Structure

Structure is the overall order of your essay. If an essay is like a tower and the different paragraphs are each a building block, the question that structure asks is: Do you have your building blocks in the best order? Is there some other approach to the overall essay and how it is put together that would make it a more compelling argument, or easier for the marker to read? Markers are people just like you. If you are having difficulty following the sequence of your argument, then chances are they will too. What can you do to fix this? This is where structure comes in.

Getting your points down on paper is the first step. Then ask yourself the question: Are they in the best order to make the most convincing case?

The other obvious question that structure considers is: Do you have the right-sized blocks in place for your essay? Essays need an introduction, body, and conclusion. Is each of these sections in place and of the size that is required? This, too, is a question of structure. You will need to know how much space to devote to an introduction, how much to the body of your essay, and how much to the conclusion (there are some suggestions on this in Chapter Five).

Coverage

Coverage means breadth. Have you read enough on this topic? Have you sufficiently covered what was required in the essay to demonstrate your understanding to the marker? Is there more work you need to do in order to more fully understand the issues? The trouble is that many of us suffer from laziness and it is tempting to NOT go and hunt for that extra book or additional piece of information. You know that you should, but you hope that perhaps it just won't be missed. Well, you are going to have to fight this impulse in writing essays. Because one of the big benefits of planning is that it should identify the things that you don't know, as well as the things you do. If you are going to answer the question correctly, this will often require more reading and gathering of additional content.

A Simple Method For Planning Your Essay

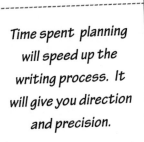

Time spent planning will speed up the writing process. It will give you direction and precision.

It is now time to start planning your essay. You have read generally on the topic and feel that you are ready to put pen to paper and put your ideas in order. How do you go about it? A method that works well and does not take much time is the paragraph method. It allows you to think about all four areas mentioned above: content, logic, structure, and coverage.

The Paragraph Method

This method, as the name suggests, is based around paragraphs. Essentially, think about the paragraph as the building block of the essay, with each paragraph 140–160 words long. If, for example, your essay is going to be 1200 words, then you have around eight paragraphs to work with.

Step one

On a blank sheet of paper draw eight boxes. Each box represents one paragraph.

Step two

Let's say that the first box is your introduction and the final box is going to be your conclusion. That leaves six boxes in the middle to fill as the body of your essay. Within each box write the main idea that you want to express in your paragraph. For example, if your subject is the Industrial

Revolution, you might have one box on changes in agriculture, one on the rise of factories, another on the drift of population from rural areas to cities, another on loss of craft skills among workers, a further box on technological advances, and a final box on the social ills caused as a result of the Industrial Revolution.

I have produced a sample box plan for you below. Have a look. Yours might be more spaced out than this; that's fine. The important thing is that you represent each paragraph as a single box.

Your Box Plan

Topic: *Industrial Revolution*

Paragraph 1 *Introduction*	Paragraph 5 *Loss of craft skills among workers*
Paragraph 2 *Changes in agriculture*	Paragraph 6 *Technological advances*
Paragraph 3 *Rise of factories*	Paragraph 7 *Social ills*
Paragraph 4 *Drift of population from rural areas to cities*	Paragraph 8 *Conclusion*

Step three

Now look at the boxes again. This time rewrite your main point as an active phrase. Do not say: 'Rise of the factories', say: 'How the rise of factories contributed to pollution and overcrowding'. Expressing your ideas like this will help you think about what the aim of your paragraph really is. It will help you think about what you are trying to convey to the reader. Based on this approach, the following is what you might write in paragraphs 4 and 6:

Paragraph 4
How the drift of population from rural areas to cities caused overcrowding and contributed to rural poverty

Paragraph 6
How technological advances in the Industrial Revolution enabled better communication

Step four

The next step is to put in some content. Not much, but enough to jog your memory and to remind you what information you are going to use in support of your main idea. In the blank space left in each box, jot down some relevant facts, examples, names, or terms that you know you would like to discuss in your paragraph. For example:

Paragraph 6
How technological advances in the Industrial Revolution enabled better communication
• Stephenson's rocket
• increase in use of roads and railroads by 1840s
• use of canals to transport goods
• advent of steam ship from 1870s

Your plan is almost complete...

Step five

The final thing to think about is structure. You have all the boxes, but are they in the best order? How could the paragraphs in the body of your essay be rearranged in order to make your argument more convincing? In the plan above, for example, wouldn't it be stronger and more logical to group all the paragraphs about factories together and put paragraph 6 after paragraphs 3 and 4, so that common ideas stick together?

For your essay, only you will know the best flow of paragraphs and how you want to develop your argument. The important thing is that you pause at this point and consider whether you need to reorder any of those boxes and present the information in a different sequence. Later, when your marker reads your essay, the thought that you gave to what you said, and the order in which you said it, will stand out.

CHAPTER THREE

Getting Down To Business

The Essay

In this chapter we look at writing the essay. Broadly, we consider the three parts of the essay—the introduction, the body, and the conclusion—and examine what each part needs to achieve. Individually, they each perform a different function in the essay. You need to learn what this is, and more importantly, how to go about writing them. We look at each in turn. Using some examples, I show you how to write the kinds of sentences that go into each part. What you will read in this chapter is a basic essay model. Learn it—it will serve you well for any of the essay writing that you face.

Of course, over time many of you will want to write more sophisticated versions. Go for it. As long as you incorporate the elements that I discuss here in your superior versions, you will be fine. But do not do this until you have learned the basics. Take some time to master the fundamentals—these are what your marker is looking

Many people do not understand what is expected of them in academic writing. If you master the fundamentals, your essays will immediately stand out from those of your peers.

for in your work. If you can learn this approach and integrate it into your own writing you will catapult yourself into the top half of the class. Naturally, some of your marks are determined by the content of your essay, but read on. If you use the method outlined here it will force you to rethink your approach to content and you will learn the kind of information that is required in essay writing, and that which is not.

The Introduction

The first part of your essay is the introduction. In a good essay, an introduction consists of a single paragraph of approximately 100 words. For longer essays—greater than 2000 words in length—there is an additional short paragraph you might wish to add to your introduction. I will discuss this shortly.

On The Question Of 'I'

Let me at the outset make a quick point about the use of 'I'. Students always ask: 'Can I use "I" in my essay? Can I say: "In this essay I will examine..."?' This is a thorny issue and one on which markers do not agree. Some accept the use of 'I' in the introduction and conclusion; others detest it and may mark you down for using it.

My recommendation is that you play it safe and learn to express yourself without using 'I'. Leave it out. You can say exactly the same thing—still conveying your opinion—in other ways.

Do not say: 'In this essay I argue that...' Instead, simply say:

- 'This essay argues that . . .'
- 'This essay will show . . .'
- 'This essay suggests that . . .'
- 'This essay examines the . . .'

You are still showing that you are about to take a side and present an opinion, but you are doing so without bringing in the first person pronoun, 'I'.

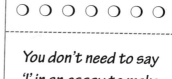

You don't need to say 'I' in an essay to make your point and your beliefs about a topic known. Learn how to make your essay speak for you.

Writing Your Introduction

Now let's get down to writing. What you need to realise from the outset is that the introduction in an academic essay contains a number of sentences, each of which performs a special function. Each has a purpose and each is necessary. You can embellish later in your career, but at this stage, if you do not have each of the following in your introduction, your essay is not yet as good as it could be and will not get you the best possible grade.

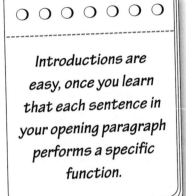

Introductions are easy, once you learn that each sentence in your opening paragraph performs a specific function.

In this section, I am going to look at each sentence in turn and follow this with an example. If you are working on an assignment at the moment, I suggest you try each as we go along. They are not hard, and if anything, you will see your assignment begin to take a firmer shape before your eyes as we progress.

Introduction: Sentence One

Sentence one is a neutral sentence that will engage the reader's interest in the essay. A neutral sentence is one that is not a point of debate. It is a sentence in which the accuracy of the facts is generally accepted. The purpose of this sentence is to ease the reader into the general area of the topic, introducing them in a non-combative way to the subject they are to read about.

For example, if your essay was on the subject of Impressionism you might say something like:

Sentence One Example: In the late nineteenth century the vibrant and colourful work of Impressionist artists transformed the art industry in Europe.

No one would disagree with such a sentence; in a simple way, it arouses your interest in the topic.

[Please note, for all the examples in this book, I am using hypothetical names and facts to illustrate sentence styles. In addition, for a full discussion on how to reference your work, see Chapter Seven.]

Introduction: Sentence Two

Your second sentence now picks up the topic you are writing about in this essay more specifically. Here you should use some of the conventional opening prompts such as 'This essay will examine...' or 'This essay will consider...' or 'This essay will discuss...'

Some students make the mistake of thinking these phrases are boring and that they need to be more creative with their introductions. This is an error. In academic writing such phrases as these are the convention. Actually, if you do not use them, you suggest to your marker your ignorance rather than your mastery of essay writing.

Go and look at some of the publications in your field and you will see that this is the case. Pick out some of the best articles written by those in the know, or some great book examining your topic, and read the first couple of paragraphs introducing their article or a chapter in their book. See if they don't use one of these phrases or a variation of one of them. I bet they do. Phrases like this in academic writing serve an important purpose: they signal to the reader that what follows is what this essay or chapter is all about.

When you read books and articles on your subject, start to pay attention to the sorts of phrases that the best writers use to express themselves.

This also means that you as the writer need to be careful about what you state in these phrases. You will be judged on whether or not you kept to what you said after one of these statements. Here's an example based on this hypothetical essay we are developing about Impressionism.

- -

Sentence Two Example: This essay will examine to what extent Impressionism was a distinct movement with recognisable characteristics and not merely an adaptation of existing art schools.

Introduction: Sentence Three

The third sentence in the introduction is quite important—it's where you put your essay in context. It's your chance to show the reader early on that you know something about your topic. You are not showing off; that is not the purpose. Instead, you are putting the reader at ease, suggesting that you have done your homework—you have read around this subject—and they can now relax and enjoy what will be an interesting and informative discussion.

Remembering that the aim is to put your particular topic in its broader context, here's the next example:

Sentence Three Example: While a number of writers, such as Chevron, Classey, and White, have argued that Impressionism was a revolution, this view is not universally held.

Introduction: Sentence Four

If you think of sentence two as the big picture sentence, and sentence three as putting the essay in context, then sentence four is the laser light bearing down on the absolute detail of your essay. Here is where you show the limitations of your essay—the boundaries of what you will be looking at—and you give away your answer. That's right. In your fourth sentence (and spilling into your fifth sentence) you explicitly state your argument in the essay and what your answer is. Do NOT leave your answer out. You must state what you are really trying to argue in your essay.

If your question allows you to take a particular side in a debate, then state here which side of the debate your essay will be arguing and on what basis. If your question allows you to take a stance on a

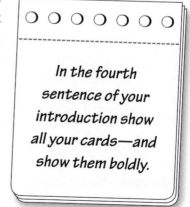

In the fourth sentence of your introduction show all your cards—and show them boldly.

subject from any one of multiple perspectives, now is the time to state which perspective you will be presenting and what your overall argument is. What is it that you want the reader to grasp: what is your point—your argument—or in fancy terms, your thesis?

Here's what the fourth sentence might look like, bringing that laser light perspective to bear on the overall topic being discussed. Note how after reading this you would be very clear what would be in this essay (and what might not be).

Sentence Four Example: Looking in detail at the work of Degas, this essay will suggest that obvious innovations appeared in Degas' work which set him apart as an artist, though a close examination reveals ties to traditional approaches in both his stylistic flair and technique.

Introduction: Sentence Five

The fifth sentence sums up. It builds on what you just said in your fourth sentence and drives it home in a clear and definitive way. Here, again, it is an acceptable convention to use phrases like 'Overall, this essay will argue...' or 'In sum,...' These phrases merely indicate to the reader that they are about to read a concluding remark that is an accurate summation of all that this essay is attempting to convey.

Sentence Five Example: Overall, this essay will argue that Impressionism was both a connection with the past and a novel innovation.

Putting It All Together

Time to make it work! If we put together all of the sentences that we have just worked on, we get the following first paragraph. Watch how the sentences build upon each other and note how they perform their function. By the end of this paragraph the reader is left in no doubt what your essay is about, and what you are going to try and convince them of in your essay. This is the purpose of the first paragraph in an academic essay.

Paragraph One Example: In the late nineteenth century the vibrant and colourful work of Impressionist artists transformed the art industry in Europe. This essay will examine to what extent Impressionism was a distinct movement with recognisable characteristics and not merely an adaptation of existing art schools. While a number of writers, such as Chevron, Classey, and White, have argued that Impressionism was a revolution, this view is not universally held. Looking in detail at the work of Degas, this essay will suggest that obvious innovations appeared in Degas' work which set him apart as an artist, though a close examination reveals ties to traditional approaches in both his stylistic flair and technique. Overall, this essay will argue that Impressionism was both a connection with the past and a novel innovation.

Have A Go

Your marker is waiting for you to produce a paragraph like this. It shows that you are mastering the craft of essay writing. Have a go. Look at the question you have to write an essay on and sketch out a series of five sentences in the form shown above. Very quickly you will see how differently your essay introductions begin to read.

Writing like this is forcing you to think about the *content* of your essay more carefully. Can you see how a specific and detailed introduction like this is making you think through what you really want to say in your essay? You need to be more precise and more accurate. No longer can you get away with using lots of descriptions or vague general terms. You are writing better introductions; but you also have to think!

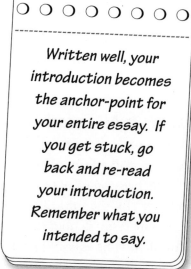

Written well, your introduction becomes the anchor-point for your entire essay. If you get stuck, go back and re-read your introduction. Remember what you intended to say.

Do Not Worry

If you are anxious at this point that producing an academic essay is about learning a sentence-by-sentence formula—relax. It is not. The introduction is the only time when we have to be so careful about each sentence. Good introductions can make or break an essay. Not only do they form the marker's first impression of you and your competence on this particular topic, the introduction lays out your whole argument. Written well, it plays a vital part in helping you order your thoughts and realise what it is that you are actually writing about.

Optional Paragraph For Longer Essays

A clear and thoughtful introduction is the first indication to the marker that you have produced a top-class essay.

If your essay is longer than 2000 words, then I suggest you add an additional 100-word paragraph to your introduction. This is particularly the case at higher levels of tertiary study where longer essays are more commonplace.

The purpose of this extra paragraph is to state the order in which your ideas are to be presented. In three or four easy sentences, you lay out the structure of your essay. Here's what it could look like:

Optional Paragraph For Longer Essay: This essay is structured in three parts. In part one, the essay will examine the roots of Impressionism in France and, in particular, among the Paris sect. Part two considers the work of Degas between 1817 and 1867, discussing the various influences that contributed to his style as an artist. Finally, part three will look more closely at Degas' technique, identifying two entirely new contributions in style he displayed as an artist, as well as three connections with more traditional art schools; each of these examples illustrating the tension between tradition and novelty in Impressionistic art.

Do not be afraid to use phrases like 'In part one...' or 'In part two ...' or 'First, this essay will...secondly, this essay will...' Such terms are accepted practice.

In addition, the choice is yours whether you call the different sections of your essay parts, or sections, or just use firstly, secondly, thirdly. The point that you are trying to get across to the reader is that this essay has logic and structure that has been carefully considered. Moreover, you have prepared the marker in a professional way for what is to follow.

For those of you writing essays shorter than 2000 words, you may add an abbreviated form of this paragraph to the end of your single opening paragraph if you wish. This is quite acceptable.

In summary, by the end of your introduction nothing about your answer is left up to the marker's imagination, and that is a good thing. However, while the marker knows your topic and the particular stance you are about to take in the essay, they do not yet know the thoughtful examples and compelling content you are about to present in support of your case. This is where the body of the essay takes over.

The Body Of The Essay
Points To Remember

If you have followed the above guide for the introduction, planning what you have to write in the body of the essay will be relatively straightforward. You will already know what the main argument of your essay is, and what each of the various sections needs to contribute to make your argument stand.

I cannot stress this enough. When a marker writes comments such as 'point?' or 'reference to question?' or 'relevance?' in the margin of your work, they are essentially saying that you have strayed from the topic. Remaining firmly within the bounds of the purpose that you set yourself in the first paragraph—or two for longer essays—remedies this problem. What you say in those paragraphs serves as a map for keeping you on course.

Always remember that an academic essay is an argument. You are building a case for one side or another. It is your job to show how the point of view that you are arguing holds water. How is it the right one?

How is it the best informed?

This does not mean that in the body of your essay you will only present information that supports the point of view that you wish to argue. A sophisticated essay will show both sides of the argument, and carefully weigh the various points of view, knowing all along which side it intends to come down on. This is part of the process of persuasion. You can show a) the strengths behind your position, and b) why an alternative position would not be tenable.

Stay within the question. You cannot afford to waste words exploring interesting issues outside your topic. You won't get marks for it.

The body of the essay is where you present your case. You deliver the points in favour of your argument and support these with detailed evidence. This is the process you now need to master.

Paragraph Structure In The Body Of The Essay

The paragraphs in the body of the essay all follow a similar type of structure. The first sentence of each paragraph should give the point you are making. The questions you need to ask yourself are: How is this paragraph relevant to the topic? What do I want the reader of this essay to understand after they read this paragraph? What am I trying to convey?

If we were following the example presented above, regarding Degas and Impressionism, and remembering that our section is to be on 'the roots of Impressionism in France and, in particular, among the Paris sect', we might write something like this for the first sentence of the first paragraph in the essay body:

- -

Sentence One Example—Body of Essay: France, and in particular Paris, was a natural birthing ground for the Impressionist movement.

- -

Here, a strong point has been made. I have stated what at this stage appears to be opinion, but in the sentences that follow I will support this with evidence to show that this statement is not just my opinion, but is in fact warranted.

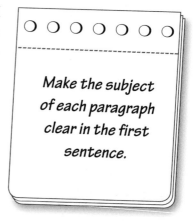

Make the subject of each paragraph clear in the first sentence.

The second sentence in your body paragraph will often work to amplify the first. It may put your idea in context. It may link your leading sentence to the essay's question. Either way, the second sentence serves to articulate further why what you have just said in sentence one was significant or related to the issue at hand. For my second sentence I might write something like:

Sentence Two Example—Body of Essay: As London was a magnet for financiers in the nineteenth century, so, too, Paris acted as a 'capital city' for the international art world, attracting painters, sculptors, and dealers from across Europe.

In the above sentence, I have tried to put my point in a broader context, but I could have tried an alternative version to stress the relevance of what I said in sentence one regarding Paris as a birthing ground:

Sentence Two Alternative—Body of Essay: Any movement, artistic or revolutionary, requires a concentration of passionate and committed individuals, and Paris—with its established art schools, art societies, and art critics—served this purpose well.

Giving Your Evidence: Sentences Three To Seven

Sentences three to seven of your body paragraph will convey evidence in support of the point you have just made. The number of sentences you write will in part depend on the length of your example, but three to five sentences is a fair guide.

What you write in these sentences is very important. These sentences are the heart of your essay—where you will gain (or lose) the most marks. Here you are revealing to the marker what you have discovered about the topic and bringing in evidence to support your arguments. There are basically three sources of evidence you can use, and good writers will use a mixture of each of these in their essays.

For each of the three sources, I will show you an example of how sentences in your paragraph might be constructed:

1. Facts And Figures

If you are to use facts and figures as the basis for supporting your point you will use things like published dates, numbers, census data, report information, summary figures, scientific data, etc. Whatever the type, you will see from the example below that the emphasis is on detail. Do not write in vague terms; be specific—be detailed. Returning to our example, if I were to write a few sentences teasing out this paragraph (and please note I am using purely hypothetical facts here for the sake of example), I might write something like:

There are three basic types of evidence you can use to make your point in an essay: facts and figures, case examples, and the insights of others. Learn them; use them. Don't leave your ideas unsupported.

Sentences Three To Five Using Facts And Figures:
The growth of art societies in Paris between 1809 and 1845 showed this strongly. Though the number of engineering societies in Paris rose from just 12 to 14 during this period, artistic societies increased from 23 to 47. By 1851, the French Census reported that artistic societies had in excess of 18,000 members drawn from all sectors of society.

Like the other examples that you are about to read, the point of this information is to support the accuracy of the claim that was made in the first sentence of this paragraph. How can someone trust my original statement, or know that I am making it with good cause, unless I support it with evidence? They cannot. So make sure that you provide good evidence, that it is related to the question at hand, and that it is specific. Go for detail—it shows that you know your material and are mounting a strong and thoughtful argument.

2. Case Examples

The second good source of evidence, and probably the one most commonly used, is actual examples of the point you have just made, or mini-case studies. For example, if you were writing a history essay you might describe the actions of a particular person, or what occurred in a specific country or city during a period of history, to amplify your point. If you were writing an English essay, you might investigate the behaviour of a particular

> *Case examples are excellent. They demonstrate your ability to find a relevant example to illustrate the point you have just made.*

character, focusing on a specific scene and that character's response to it. If you were writing an economics essay or a business essay, you might look at the example of a particular country or a particular firm and how the problem you are discussing affected them.

Whatever the source, you are going to present an example that is relevant to the point you are making and which serves to illustrate the strength of your argument. Using this approach, and keeping with our theme of Impressionism, here is what these sentences would look like:

Body Paragraph Using Case Examples: One of the many people to come to Paris during this period was Pierre Rodin. Originally from Antwerp, Rodin brought with him not only his love of art, but also his strong connections to the Dutch art trade. Commencing a gallery on the Left Bank of the Seine in 1816, he invested 24,000 francs in early Impressionist art between 1816

and 1819, and his enthusiastic patronage assisted many early
artists while attracting still further Parisian painters to try their
hand at Impressionism.

- -

3. The Insights And Writings Of Somebody Else

The third source of evidence is to use what someone else has said about
your point. Here, the 'somebody else' is usually a scholar or academic
who has written on the topic and whose point of view you wish to use in
support of your argument. What you will be doing for the next three to
five sentences is paraphrasing their work and discussing how it is relevant
or supportive of what you are trying to say. (For some more examples of
this approach, see Chapter Six.)

- -

Sentences Using An Authority: Historian James Claver suggests
that Paris, more than any other European centre, in the early
part of the nineteenth century, was a melting pot of artistic
talent. In looking at six of the main cities in Europe, Claver
identified that only Paris had an existing artistic community
which sustained both schools for the training of future
artists, as well as societies to provide for their welfare and
encouragement. Claver states: 'Paris was a central focus for a
well-connected French artistic brotherhood.'

- -

[Note: In each of the above examples, where specific quotes or facts
are given, or the work of others is referred to, you will need to correctly
reference your source. How to do this is discussed in Chapter Seven.]

Each of the three forms of paragraph above performs the same
function: it serves to convey evidence in support of the point that you
clearly and unambiguously stated in your first sentence.

Two Absolutely Vital Things To Remember

1. Be Specific With Your Evidence

Look at the sentences I have written. I did not speak in vague terms
about the growing interest in art in Paris. Instead, I used specific names
and dates. I gave amounts of money and facts—I was precise and

detailed. This gives your essay reliability, credibility, and depth.

If you cannot back something up with specific, interesting, relevant evidence, do not say it. Or, say it differently so that you can. Do not make vague, generalised statements.

2. Ensure Each Paragraph Has Only One Point

In each of the paragraphs I wrote above there was only one point, and the evidence I gave served to illustrate or support that ONE point. If you want to make a further point, write another paragraph. Do not clutter your paragraphs with additional things that you might want to say, which ultimately only detract from the one thing that you were saying well.

The Final Sentence

The final sentence of your paragraph may do one of several things. It may restate or emphasise what you have just said; it may refer back to the main question of the essay so there is no confusion in the mind of the reader; it may conclude with a strong comment about the topic of the paragraph; or it may serve as a connecting sentence, offering an easy link into the paragraph that is to follow. Any of these make viable final sentences and all are employed by good writers, especially the use of linking sentences. To restate our point, and drive it home, we might write something like:

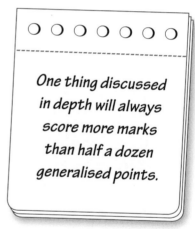

One thing discussed in depth will always score more marks than half a dozen generalised points.

- -
Final Sentence: Body Paragraph: With such a strong base on which to draw, it is not surprising that new movements like Impressionism could find a natural core of supporters and talent in Paris.
- -

Don't Forget Linking Sentences

Too often, essay writers forget that they are not just crafting a dozen well-balanced paragraphs, but that each of these paragraphs makes up a whole, and the reader likes to be led through the forest of ideas with comforting little remarks, so they know that they are still on the right pathway.

The following types of lines could be used: 'Having considered the work of Claver we now turn to the next important period in the life of ...' Or something like, 'But colour was not the only central fact in Degas' success, his choice of portrait also played a part...' Or 'The next important chapter in the life of ...'

Alternatively, you may employ the following very reliable structuring device: 'There were three aspects. Firstly, Degas worked feverishly for long periods without food or human company. Secondly, having completed the draft of a work, he seldom put it down unfinished. Thirdly, ...'

Any construction like this does the same thing: it helps to lead the reader gently and logically through your essay and reassures them that you knew what you were doing when you wrote it.

Overall, a body paragraph complete with all its sentences might look like the example below. This one uses the mini-case study example shown previously. See how each of the sentences serves to support the others and how the main point of the paragraph is rammed home

Remember, your essay is a work to be read from start to finish. Don't lose your reader. Lead them through your ideas by using linking sentences.

by the use of the relevant example. The conclusion states solidly to the reader that what the paragraph hoped to achieve has been realised:

Complete Paragraph—Body of Essay: France, and in particular Paris, was a natural birthing ground for the Impressionist movement. As London was a magnet for financiers in the nineteenth century, so, too, Paris acted as a 'capital city' for the international art world, attracting painters, sculptors, and dealers from across Europe. One of the many people to come to Paris during this period was Pierre Rodin. Originally from Antwerp, Rodin brought with him not only his love of art, but also his strong connections to the Dutch art trade. Commencing a gallery on the Left Bank of the Seine in 1816, he invested 24,000 francs in early Impressionist art between 1816 and 1819, and his enthusiastic patronage assisted many early artists while attracting still further Parisian painters to try their hand at Impressionism. With such a strong base on which to draw, it is not surprising that new movements like Impressionism could find a natural core of supporters and talent in Paris.

The Conclusion

Many people find writing the conclusion of their essay difficult. They wonder what to say, thinking that they have already said all that they want to in the body of the essay—so what is there left to say in the conclusion? 'Won't my conclusion be dull and boring?' The answer is 'No'. Conclusions are not dull and boring. Like the introduction, they have a particular purpose and there are a number of interesting ways to write conclusions that can make them one of the most thoughtful and enjoyable parts of the essay to write.

The best place to start when you are thinking about what to write in your conclusion is your introduction. Go back and re-read what you said about the intent of your essay. What did you say you would accomplish or demonstrate or prove in this essay? This is information you must restate in your conclusion—but the subtle difference is that you are not only going to emphasise what you have proven, but also how you have proven it.

Let's look again at the sample essay on Impressionism and begin to work up a conclusion that brings in these ideas. To start off, we might write something along the lines of:

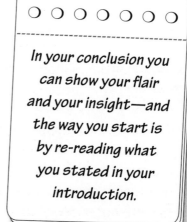

In your conclusion you can show your flair and your insight—and the way you start is by re-reading what you stated in your introduction.

Conclusion: First Sentences: This essay has considered to what extent Impressionism was a distinct movement with recognisable characteristics and not merely an adaptation of existing art schools. Examining, in particular, the work of Degas, it has shown that while there were innovations in Degas' painting which gave it a unique quality, evidence presented here demonstrates that there were strong ties to more traditional artistic schools and approaches.

Now, having written this, give your conclusion a twist to make it interesting and to demonstrate to the marker just how much you have thought about this topic. Tell them what the most significant point in your essay was. Not all the information that you have presented was of equal worth. Look at it carefully and decide which evidence was the most significant. Of all the facts, which stood out as contributing more to your answer than anything else? Whose opinion would you give the most credence to from among those that you considered?

In short, stand back from your essay for a moment and think about its relative merits and then state which points you felt were strongest (or which were weakest). By doing so, you are demonstrating your ability to make judgements over your research material. This is one of the abilities that top students cultivate. Make it yours.

Your final paragraph might look like the one shown below:

Conclusion Paragraph Example: This essay has considered to what extent Impressionism was a distinct movement with recognisable characteristics and not merely an adaptation of existing art schools. Examining in particular the work of Degas, it has shown that while there were innovations in Degas' painting which gave it a unique quality, evidence presented here has demonstrated that there were strong ties to more traditional artistic schools and approaches. However, not all the influences on Degas' work were equal. While clearly the Parisian artistic sect played a dominant role on his work throughout his life, this essay has shown that the pervasive influence of the Dutch art dealer Pierre Rodin, and his contacts in the European art trade, quickly enabled Degas and other painters to find a commercial outlet for their work. Overall, it appears that financial gain, just as much as a love of taste, influenced how, and what, the Impressionists painted.

Note how, at the end of the conclusion, you can draw on the evidence you have presented in the body of your essay to restate your argument in an interesting and forceful way. You do not need to suggest that you have the final and conclusive answer, but you can qualify your answer. In the final sentence, with the phrase 'it appears', I am not suggesting that my essay is the last word on Impressionism, but that on the basis of what I have presented in my essay, I believe my point has merit. This is what you do in your conclusion.

Do not introduce new information, but demonstrate to the marker that you can think through what you have written about in an insightful and analytical way.

Points For Your Conclusion

Here are some points to think about that you might like to comment on in your conclusion. Don't try and put them all in, but pick one or two to add a twist and show your analytical ability:

- What are the most important or significant points in your essay?
- What key themes appeared in your essay—and how did these group or develop over the course of the essay?
- Was there a surprising piece of evidence that stands out—a mini-case study or quote—that really exemplified the overall argument you were trying to make? Does this make you reinterpret, or understand in a deeper way, some of the other evidence you presented?
- Of all the evidence you presented, which is the weakest and why?
- What are some of the possible flaws/limitations in your argument?
- What further information would you like to consider before you could make a more informed judgement?

- Of all the experts that you considered in your essay, who do you think had the strongest opinion and why?
- What is the most pertinent fact and/or figure?
- How might your claims change in the future? What might make them change?

Merely describing what you have done is lower-order thinking. Prioritising, making informed judgements, qualifying your assertions—these demonstrate your ability to think at a deeper level.

CHAPTER FOUR

The Sentence: Exposed And Explained

Sentences are the core of your essay and most of us think that we're not bad at writing them. But there are several traps. Often, we either write sentences that are far too long, or we do not know how to write different types of sentences. In this chapter we will consider both of these issues. Firstly, we will look at 12 different sentence styles that you can write. Some are variations on sentence openings; others are different ways to structure your sentences. These will give your work variety and make it more interesting to read and, most importantly, you will learn to express yourself and your ideas more convincingly. Secondly, we will look at the ideal length of a sentence and why some of your present work may be difficult to follow.

Leave The Simple Sentence Behind

Before we look at the different sentence styles, read the following (hypothetical) paragraph. See if you can spot the flaw:

- -

Economic growth varies from country to country. Japan, however, has enjoyed a growth beyond many comparable nations. The GDP in the 1980s was almost twice her nearest OECD partner and that was not all. Entrepreneurs emerged all over Japan fuelling this fire of industrial expansion. Sam Kabuki was one example. He commenced with only a small trading store in Tokyo in 1981, and within four years had expanded to 35 branches with offices in New York and Paris. *The Economist* magazine named him entrepreneur of the decade. It was a large surprise then, when in 1995, he fell from grace and was quickly bankrupt.

- -

I am sure you can spot many areas for improvement, but the major flaw is the type of sentence used. They are all basically *simple sentences* and begin with the subject of the sentence every time. Here are some more:

- The dog ran across the road.
- Charlie was his name.
- He was a friendly dog.
- It was good to know him.
- Roads must always be crossed carefully.

Can you see it now? You can thinly disguise them by placing 'It' in front, or leading off with nouns like 'Charlie' or 'Roads', but these sentences are all of the same type. Like any style of sentence which is overused, they quickly become boring and repetitive.

Now look at the paragraph again. Same subject and information, only this time I have varied the styles of sentence used.

- -

Economic growth varies from country to country. Japan, however, has enjoyed a growth beyond many comparable nations. Among the OECD nations, Japan's GDP in the 1980s was almost twice her nearest OECD partner. That was not all. Emerging all over Japan, entrepreneurs fuelled this fire of industrial expansion. Sam Kabuki was one example. Incredibly, he commenced with only a small trading store in Tokyo in 1981; yet, within four years, had expanded to 35 branches with offices in New York and Paris. When one of the world's top financial

papers—*The Economist*—named him entrepreneur of the
decade, his 1995 bankruptcy came as a shock.

Same information, only said in a more interesting fashion. None
of this is hard to master, but better essay writers vary the style of
sentence they use to keep the reader interested in their writing and
their arguments crisp. Here are *12 sentence styles* you can practise and
quickly incorporate into your paragraphs for greater impact and interest.

1. The Very Short Sentence

This one is often overlooked, yet is so easy to use. Use five or six words at
most. No more. Keep it short and make it punchy. In your paragraphs
the very short sentence can break up a longer flow of ideas where you
fear the reader may be losing interest, or, if you have an argument that is
moving slowly toward its central point and you want to make a statement
that the reader will not miss, an effective weapon is to drop in a very short
sentence. The impact is immediate. You have the reader's attention. See?

2. Repeating Pattern

Again, these are easy to use but, like any of these sentence styles, don't
overplay them otherwise they will tend to wear out their welcome. While
you can use very short sentences at the rate of about one per paragraph,
you are going to have to use the repeating pattern a little more sparingly.
The method is to pick one aspect of your sentence and use it as a motif,
repeating it several times over for effect. You can choose either a single
word in the sentence or a short phrase. Either will work.

Here are a couple of examples:

- Without doubt, the most vibrant economy was Japan, and the
  most vibrant entrepreneur in that economy was Sam Kabuki.
- Adding texture to his painting was smart; adding to his financial
  commitments was not so clever.
- The rise was great, the downfall was even greater.
- It did not hurt, it did not matter.
- The team found it difficult to raise the money, though not as
  difficult to lose it.

3. Adverb At The Front

This is one of the simplest styles to use, and can quickly alter a plain sentence into one that has a bit more interest and texture. Subtly, you drop in an adverb at the start of the sentence to introduce it. Cleverly, it changes the flow of your paragraph and you can use the adverb to accentuate a particular point that you are trying to make. So, if ever you get stuck for how you might introduce a sentence, grab an adverb and stick it at the front.

Adverbs: Here Are a Few... subsequently, immediately, shortly, always, frequently, previously, carefully, thoughtfully, readily, thankfully, however, therefore, moreover, fortunately, yet, seldom, pleasantly, surprisingly, probably, frankly, often, subsequently, deliberately, steadily, expertly, erratically, foolishly, almost, thoroughly, earlier, profoundly, easily, noticeably, still, even, indeed, remarkably, meanwhile

----

Importantly, the adverb you use at the front of a sentence should always be followed by a comma. This is the rule.

Here are some examples:

- Quickly, the company regrouped and launched a further product on the market.
- Firstly, this essay discusses the issue of musical interpretation in the sixteenth century.
- Interestingly, pottery was not discovered first in Cornwall.
- Initially, she hesitated before committing the full resources of the organisation.
- Habitually, Coleridge used metaphors to express the deeper points in his poetry.
- Carefully, Bismarck extended his influence into Austrian politics.
- Suddenly, their fortunes changed irreversibly.

4. The Em Dash

This is one of my personal favourites. The em dash (—) is classy and you can really have some fun in a paragraph throwing in a good em dash sentence. The function of the em dash in written English is to isolate a section of a sentence where a phrase is inserted that the writer wants included in the sentence, but the phrase is oblique to the natural flow or content of that sentence. Have a look at a couple of examples, and you will quickly see what I mean:

- The London Stock Exchange—premier of all the world's financial markets—quickly regained its composure as trading improved.
- His style as a musician was awkward—a clumsy and undignified sort of demeanour—and the other players soon grew tired of his precocious ways.

Or, for something quite polished, try the stylish em dash at the start of the sentence:

- Daring, graceful, unforgettable—the sleek blue convertible slid out of the driveway and seamlessly entered the flow of traffic.

5. The 'W' Start

Try a 'W' start to a sentence. It's easy to use and always adds interest to the flow of your argument. Some easy 'W's' to remember: When, Where, What, Why, Who, or the 'Th' posing as a 'W'—Though. Here are some examples:

- Where other musicians failed, he excelled.
- When he entered the room, the crowd cheered enthusiastically.
- Why he was not at his best in his final campaign before he died is a mystery.
- Who was responsible for the fall in currency prices was not the main question.
- Though many other writers have tried to emulate Dickens, few have come close.

6. The Paired-Double

It is far too easy to overuse 'and' in sentences. You are in the flow of an idea and want to add a further point just to make it complete. Or, you have in your mind one thing, when suddenly you think of something else and just must add it to the sentence before it slips out of your mind altogether. The result is a series of chaotic 'ands' that litter your paragraphs and quickly tire the reader.

Get rid of them. Use the semi-colon; that's what it is designed for.

If you have two independent clauses—two clauses which can stand as sentences by themselves—don't use 'and' to join them; use a semi-colon instead. It is more forceful and it demonstrates greater command over your writing. Here are some examples:

- *Don't say:* He was a great painter and he tried hard to make a living in his early years.
- *Say:* He was a great painter; he tried hard to make a living in his early years.
- *Don't say:* From the merchant came a volley of insults and from the prince came silence.
- *Say:* From the merchant came a volley of insults; from the prince came silence.
- *Don't say:* It was hard to earn money because it was raining in the valley all through the harvest.
- *Say:* It was hard to earn money; it was raining in the valley all through the harvest.

7. Prepositional Phrase

Open your sentence with a prepositional phrase. A preposition is a word that goes at the head of a phrase, typically a noun phrase, which modifies that phrase in some way. Often, prepositions indicate movement or position. Classic examples are by, with, from. But there are many more examples:

Prepositions: Here Are a Few...in, against, before, between, over, behind, within, under, below, herein, at, for, throughout, near, to, above, below, about, of, since, although, after, during, unlike, until, upon, despite, regardless, because, prior

---

Use one of these in a phrase at the front of your sentence. They quickly spice up your writing and give it added interest and movement. Here are a few examples (the first is a classic):

- In the beginning, God created the Heavens and the Earth.

- From the outset, it was clear it was going to be a difficult month.
- By this time, Harry knew it was going to turn out well.
- Regardless of the cost, she was determined to purchase the painting.
- Since it was not available, he wrote to the firm asking for a replacement part.
- Beneath the counterclaims and political squabbling, a far greater threat was looming.

8. Verb At The Start

Try opening your sentence with a verb. This again adds interest and movement to your writing, and any paragraph will easily take a couple of sentences of this sort. There are two forms of verbs that work well in this way: either an -ed form of the verb, or an -ing form of the verb. Have a look at these examples and try some in your writing:

- Leaving his apprenticeship, da Vinci began to paint his own commissions.
- Starting from a position of strength, the organisation soon commanded a large market.
- Walking toward the door, he quickly exited the room.
- Surveying the range of English poets who emerged in the eighteenth century, only three stood out.
- Shaken by the episode, she soon recovered.
- Questioned over the usefulness of the breakthrough, the scientist demonstrated its worth for all to see.
- Determined to pursue nothing else, she concentrated on the work until it was finished.
- Turned into a play, the account quickly drew wide praise.
- Beaten by his enemies, Napoleon retreated to the palace.

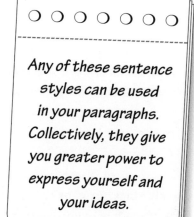

Any of these sentence styles can be used in your paragraphs. Collectively, they give you greater power to express yourself and your ideas.

9. Alliteration

Alliteration—repeating words of the same letter or sound—can be used to draw attention to a particular point. However, although it works, it should not be used more than once every couple of paragraphs as readers will tire of it. So, while I might say that 'likeable and loveable' are particularly warm descriptors and used like this they tend to work, if I use the 'marvellously mesmerising magician', you realise that alliteration has been overplayed. In short, careful, conscientious use of alliteration can work for emphasis, but not too much.

10. Metaphor And Simile

A metaphor is a figure of speech suggesting that one thing is in fact something else. A simile is a figure of speech comparing two things, saying that something is like the other.

Both have their place in non-fiction writing for academic essays. Metaphors work well for effect—they can add drama and emphasis to a description. Similes work particularly well for explaining difficult concepts and drawing analogies. Here are some examples:

- Like a prowling lion, he waited for the optimal moment to launch his campaign.
- As quick as a fox, he ran to the door.
- The lawyer grilled the witness relentlessly.
- The idea soared spectacularly once it had been given full flight.

11. Colon: And Flow

The function of the colon in written English is to act as an indicator that a point just made in a sentence is to be expanded upon. There are two common types. The first is when you wish to convey several points of information in a sentence form. Each phrase following the colon is separated by a semi-colon. Here are a couple of examples:

- There were three things that the speaker wished to discuss: firstly, the lack of leadership; secondly, the order of the meeting; thirdly, the supper menu.
- The new plane has four advantages: it flies well; it lands perfectly; it is comfortable to ride; it is relatively inexpensive.

The second type is when you wish to amplify or expand on a key word in the sentence, which is typically the *final word* in the main clause. This can be used for effect, and to allow a fuller description of a particular characteristic. Have a look at these:

- The ship left the port on time: three minutes after noon on the seventh day of December.
- It was late in the afternoon when she heard the news: Italy had won.
- The speech had a clear intent: to inform and not entertain.
- She finally remembered the title of the book: *The Laughing Professor*.

12. Good Ol' Red, White, And Blue

This is a fitting place to finish off our 12 different sentence styles, because this type of sentence is widely used. The sentence uses what some call the 'serial comma', and others call the 'Oxford comma'. The best way to remember it is to think of 'red, white, and blue'.

The problem is simple: you have three ideas which you want to convey in a sentence. These ideas are examples of what you are writing about. To do this requires the use of commas to separate the three terms accurately. The rule is red, white, and blue.

Some get this wrong. They leave out the second comma, which immediately implies a stronger relationship between the second and third terms. If this is what you wish, so be it. However, if all three items have equal merit or worth, use the serial comma. Here are some examples. The first two use the serial comma at the end of the sentence, the second pair use the serial comma to describe terms within a sentence—watch how the comma is used:

- The car was stylish, white, and expensive.
- He wanted to write well, to write clearly, and to write with impact.
- The grass was soft, green, and lush on the hillside.
- The year 1815 was a memorable one for the emperor, his army, and his government as their downfall was imminent.

Acceptable Sentence Length

The lengths of your sentences will vary. Partly, it depends on the material you are working with, your style, the emphasis you want to create, and your ability with punctuation. However, this said, one of the habitual mistakes that people make in essay writing is to write sentences that are just preposterously too long, going far beyond their own abilities, as well as the reading ability of the average marker, who often gets little sleep, especially when she or he has to wade through handwriting that is more a scrawl than intelligible English and is faced with ridiculously long sentences from students who erroneously think that they have the literary talent of Dickens but who would do far better to learn that writing long sentences is something that they should avoid at every turn and at all possible costs because inevitably, you, and the point that you were trying to make, get hopelessly lost in a flurry of commas and nonsense phrases, as you realise far too late that this is a sentence you should never have started. Get the point?!

If you want to make your writing clear, write sentences of *20 words* or less. You might think that is not very much. But you immediately improve the clarity and comprehension of your writing. Short sentences do not mean boring writing. Indeed, the complete opposite.

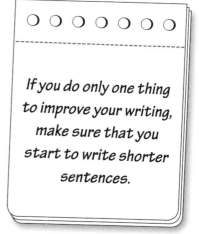

If you do only one thing to improve your writing, make sure that you start to write shorter sentences.

Twenty words actually makes quite a long sentence—typically, almost two lines of typed work. It is plenty of words to make your point and make it well before going on to the next thought (that was 20 words).

Learn the different sentence styles above—integrate them into your work—and you will start to write more interesting text. Remember, the aim is to get better marks for your essays. Varying the sentence styles that you use can help you convey your ideas effectively and intelligently. Sentences of 20 words or less will make it easier for the marker to grasp the point you are trying to get across.

CHAPTER FIVE

A Question Of Structure

How do you structure your essay? Every student asks this question at some point. In this chapter we unpack structuring and look at it in several ways. Firstly, we consider how you might structure essays of different lengths, and I give you some suggested outlines for essays of varying lengths, between 1500 and 5000 words. Secondly, we look at how the question that you are asked influences the way you structure your essay.

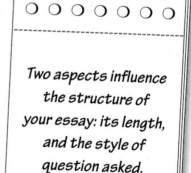

Two aspects influence the structure of your essay: its length, and the style of question asked.

We scrutinise four different question styles—all common in academic essays—to see what the marker is looking for within each of these questions. I give you some clues as to how each answer might be structured so that you stay on topic and use your words appropriately.

You will also learn some expressions of academic shorthand, and see how to avoid common errors that others make by misinterpreting questions. Finally, we will consider how to advantage yourself when you write your essay question—both in your choice of words, and in how many points you choose to cover.

Structure And Length

As discussed in Chapter One, all academic essays have three parts: an introduction, a body, and a conclusion. Yet, knowing that is not quite enough. You get assigned essays of different lengths, with different types of questions, and examiners use different sorts of words—'critically', 'describe', 'analyse', 'identify'. What does it all mean and how do you structure the different parts of your essay? In this chapter I cover all these points, but firstly, let's dispense with the question of length.

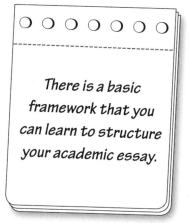

There is a basic framework that you can learn to structure your academic essay.

As a suggested guide, I have listed below some of the more frequent essay lengths, with the corresponding number of words that you should devote to the introduction, body of the essay, and the conclusion.

There are two things to bear in mind before you read this list. Firstly, it is only a guide. Having taught at four universities across two countries, I know that the breakdown below is pretty robust—but if you are concerned, check with your course lecturer.

Secondly, if you like to think in pages more than words, figure on about 400 words of typed text per page. This is about average if you are using a 12 point font, 1.5 line spacing, and a conventional font type, such as Times New Roman, Arial, Garamond, or any similar typeface.

Here are some common essay lengths and possible structures:

1500-Word Essay
- 100-word introduction
- 1200-word body of essay
- 200-word conclusion

2000-Word Essay
- 100-word introduction
- 1600-word body of essay
- 300-word conclusion

3000-Word Essay
- 200-word introduction
- 2400-word body of essay
- 400-word conclusion

5000-Word Essay
- 200-word introduction
- 4300-word body of essay
- 500-word conclusion

You can see that with the longer essays you are increasingly allowed more room to develop your introductions, as well as more words to present a thorough and well-thought-through conclusion. However, essay length is only part of the answer in deciding the appropriate structure for your essay. The next factor to take into account is the type of question that is asked, as different questions direct you to apportion the body of your essay differently. Here are some.

Deciphering Questions

Teachers and lecturers ask many different types of questions. Here, I am going to deal with a few of the more common formats used, and explain what the lecturer is looking for in the answer. I am not so concerned about the content of the answer here, as about what the essay might look like in terms of length and approach.

Pure Description

Describe two theories of human development. (2000 words)

These kinds of questions are not difficult to answer. Certainly, the structure you adopt is quite straightforward. Whatever your word length, you should ensure that you give each of the theories (or whatever subject you are asked to describe) equal coverage in your essay. For example, if your essay was 2000 words long, and you had to cover two theories, I would allocate 100 words for the introduction, 300 words for the conclusion, and then divide the remaining 1600 words evenly between the two theories, describing each as best I could.

   Similarly, if I was asked to describe three things in my essay, I would merely split the 1600 words of the body equally between each of the

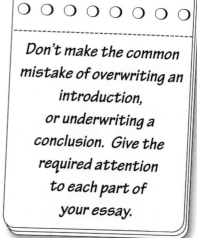

Don't make the common mistake of overwriting an introduction, or underwriting a conclusion. Give the required attention to each part of your essay.

three topics or subjects.

A variation on this type of question is this:

Describe two theories of human development. Of these, which do you feel is the most important and why? (2000 words)

This variation is asking for you to make an informed judgement. The style of question is purposely pushing you beyond mere description to a more analytical answer. Here, unless told otherwise, I would treat the question as per the 'double-whammy' question explained below. I would give 800 words to describing the two theories, then spend the next 800 words making a case for which I felt was the most important and why.

Remember, I do not make my case in the essay from merely what I think about the theories. Using the three sources of evidence (as described in Chapter Three), I would show the strengths and weaknesses of the different theories (or whatever idea or topic was being discussed), then come to an informed position as to which I believed was the most important and why.

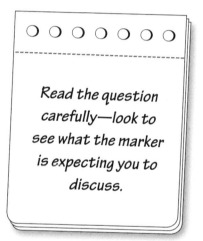

Read the question carefully—look to see what the marker is expecting you to discuss.

The Double-Whammy

What is nationalism and why is it important? Using examples, show how rising nationalism can contribute to political instability. (2000 words)

I call this one the 'double-whammy': it is one question, but it has two distinct parts. These questions demand that you are succinct with your words, given that there are two sub-questions to answer. But on a positive note, the *structure* of your essay is decided by the *form of the question*.

Unless your instructor tells you otherwise, assume that half of your essay should be devoted to the first sentence in the question, and the other half of the essay to the second sentence. Thus, for the above question, if I had to write a 2000-word essay, I would apportion 100 words for the introduction and 300 words for the conclusion. Then, I would split the remaining 1600 words evenly, answering firstly, in 800 words, 'What is nationalism and why is it important?', and secondly, in the next 800 words, 'how rising nationalism can lead to political instability'.

The best clue as to when NOT to split a question like this is if the examiner uses the word 'briefly'—this is academic shorthand for 'do not spend long on this point'.

For example, if the above question had read:

Briefly explain nationalism and why it is important. Using examples, show how rising nationalism can contribute to political instability. (2000 words)

I would have spent only one or two paragraphs in my essay explaining nationalism and its importance, because I knew that what the marker really wanted me to concentrate on was the second part of the question.

The Think Critical

Critically analyse the use of central banking measures to control the monetary supply. Your answer should make use of relevant research and the literature. (2000 words)

'Critically analyse' is academic shorthand for 'discuss the merits and shortcomings of an idea using research as your source of evidence'. What the marker is looking for here is for you to find relevant research on the topic, read it, then discuss in depth the merits and shortcomings of two or three central banking measures which can be used to control the monetary supply. We know it is only two or three 'central banking measures' because of the length of the essay question.

To discuss anything in depth, you need at least a page. So, if you do the maths for this question: allocate 100 words for the introduction, 300 words for the conclusion, which leaves you 1600 words. If you are going to discuss any issue or point in depth you are going to need a whole page, with approximately 400 words per page. In sum, you might critically analyse three central banking measures using about 550 words each, or just two, using 800 words each. Either would be acceptable.

The fundamental thing to remember here is that this sort of question is looking for an in-depth and well-argued answer. This is the classic courtroom-type question. That is, imagine you are both the defence lawyer *and* the prosecution lawyer. Your job here is to lay out both sides of the argument, strengths and weaknesses, and come to an informed judgement at the end. It may be that one form is clearly superior to all the others (based on the research that you find and present). It may be that some hybrid of two of them is best. It may be that the evidence you find holds all of them equally. Any of these combinations are acceptable answers if you have shown them on the basis of evidence.

The Quote

'All people are born equal.' Discuss. (2000 words)

This is a popular style of question. The lecturer has picked some pertinent quote from the course and set it as an essay topic. Don't be afraid that the question seems so broad that it could mean anything. These are not difficult questions to answer. What your marker is really saying is this:

Here is a thought-provoking quote. I know you are all great students and I want to see what you can do with this. I do not have a set answer in my mind. I can see at least a dozen possible ways to answer this question and all equally well. I want to give you a chance to shine. Use this quote and show me how you can explore it in a creative way, using the evidence and ideas we have discussed in the course.

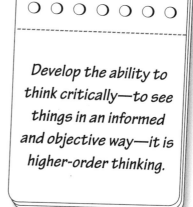

Develop the ability to think critically—to see things in an informed and objective way—it is higher-order thinking.

The key with a question like this is to take it by the horns in the first paragraph (even the first sentence) and declare from the outset how you intend to tackle the question in the essay. Here is an example:

'All people are born equal' is an enticing ideal, but in reality
does not occur. This essay will examine the ways in which
parents' educational background and the opportunities given
to children in their developmental years can quickly distance
any supposed equality at birth. In particular, this essay will
discuss the effect of . . .

One of the problems many students have with these types of question
is that they are daunted by the potential size of the topic. The question
seems so large that they do not know where to start, or how on earth
they might answer a topic of this scale in 2000 words or less. Let me
give you a strategy to manage such a dilemma.

Writing Qualifying Sentences

You can use this technique with just about any essay, but it is especially
useful with those essays where you feel the topic is so large that you are
concerned about being penalised for not covering something that you
should have. Or, you feel you could not possibly cover all of this material
in one essay. Say, for example, you were asked to:

Discuss the development of Greek culture from 500 BC to 300 BC, identifying key influences. (2000 words)

The development of Greek culture is an enormous topic and anyone
would think: How am I going to do all this in 2000 words? Well, the
trick is that you do not. You do a part of it in detail, as an example
of the broader topic. In the introductory paragraph of your essay you
write the following qualifying sentence (you might insert it as sentence
two or three in the introduction).

The development of ancient Greek culture is a broad
topic encompassing language, religion, education, dress,
architecture, literature, art, and music. For the purposes of
this essay, I will examine architecture and language as two
examples of Greek cultural development through this period.

Or, say you had something like this:

Examine how managers can increase employee motivation in the workplace. (2000 words)

Again, there are multiple techniques available for managers to improve motivation (which you could never do justice to in a 2000-word essay). To remedy this you insert a qualifying sentence. You might say something like:

Managers can increase employee motivation in many ways, such as different leadership styles, group interaction, pay and reward systems, employee feedback, objective setting, and improved working conditions. This essay will consider two of these incentives in depth—employee feedback and improved working conditions—as effective methods to raise motivation levels among staff.

By doing this you acknowledge to your marker that you comprehend the range of issues in the subject, but you also declare that you are going to answer it in a mature and deeper way.

Broad questions give you flexibility in your approach. But you need to take control of your answer from the outset.

If you want to perform in the top group of the class you need to adopt this strategy. Your marker is looking for depth of understanding—not that you can describe 15 different motivation systems in 2000 words. They want to see that you can progress from description to analysis. That is, make the move from just describing the aspects of a subject to analysing different perspectives and arriving at an informed judgement.

The C-grade essay is the one that merely describes; the A-grade essay describes and then analyses: it discusses, critiques, and presents an informed view in a focused way.

Get focused. Don't discuss 15 different aspects of your topic in a

2000-word essay; discuss two or three aspects in depth. Show what different writers or researchers think about the same issue. Discuss how that particular issue has been dealt with in different countries, or by different organisations, or in different time periods. Go for depth, not breadth. When you write your first book of 100,000 words, then you can go for breadth.

The Question As A Motif

It is heartbreaking as a marker to read an essay that is superbly written and uses good evidence, but does not answer the question set. There are two frequent causes of this mistake, both of which are avoidable.

The first error is that some students fail to read a 'double-whammy' question correctly. They talk about one part of the question, and then deal with the second part of the question merely in the conclusion, or as a kind of side thought. As a marker you are hamstrung. Even if you wanted to give the essay top marks you cannot, because the person has not addressed both parts of the question. Of course, now you know about 'double-whammies' there is no way you will fall for this again.

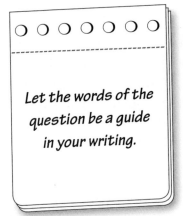

Let the words of the question be a guide in your writing.

The second error is caused when students rewrite the question in their own words. Often they do it in the introduction. They take part of the question and style it in the way they would like it to read.

Unfortunately, in the process, they can replace the words of the question with other words that do not mean the same thing. Stick to the question that the lecturer or teacher has asked and use *their* words.

In fact, I suggest one further thing. Use the words of the question as a motif in the essay. That is, as a recurring theme or phrase throughout the essay. So, for example, if the question asked you to: 'Identify the causes of the Great Depression', use the word 'cause' throughout your essay. Each time you introduce a new 'cause' call it that. Don't call it something else. Use the word that the marker has used: call it a 'cause'.

Doing this will achieve two things in your essay. Firstly, from your point of view, it is an aid to staying on the topic. Using the words of the question forces you to keep writing the essay toward answering the topic and there is less likelihood that you will stray from the subject.

Secondly, using words that the marker used in their question can help you achieve higher grades—because the words in the question act as beacons to the marker. Of course, the marker will read your whole essay, and consider it as a holistic piece of work. But think: often they mark a hundred or more essays. If your essay has clearly and smartly used a word or a phrase from the question as a recurring motif, it is far easier for the marker to recognise this when you are presenting your well-constructed arguments. When they finish reading your essay and say to themselves: 'Did this person answer the question?' the very clear answer in their head will be 'Yes'.

How Many Points To Cover?

If you take anything from this chapter I hope that you realise that the best essays are not those that rush through a dozen different points. Instead, they are written by students like you, who realise that the way to a higher mark is by covering less ground, but covering that ground in depth. These essays talk about two or three things—issues, main points, key topics, perspectives—and discuss them in depth. This does not mean lengthy descriptions. It means using evidence to move to the position of critical analysis and informed judgement in your writing. This is quite within your grasp. In the following chapter I am going to give you some more techniques to make this process as easy as possible.

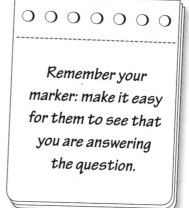

Remember your marker: make it easy for them to see that you are answering the question.

CHAPTER SIX

Style And You

Using appropriate language, you can express what you want to say in an academic essay, in a way that is essentially you.

This chapter considers a very common question among students writing essays: 'Where can I express my opinion?' You have something that you want to say, but you are not sure how to say it in an essay form, or if your views actually count for anything in an academic essay. Here we demystify the process. I will show you how to put across what you want to say in a convincing manner. We will also look at how to use other people's opinions to advantage, and how to use quotes. Finally, we will consider how to weigh evidence in your essay and deal with both the positive and negative sides of an argument in a constructive way.

The Role Of Opinion

It is very common to feel a bit frustrated by the thought of writing an academic essay. You look at the question and feel as if your job is merely to regurgitate material that has already been discovered by a whole lot of people. Where is the essential you in all this? Where can you express your opinion?

The good news is that there are many places that you can express your individuality, perceptiveness, and skill, such as:

- the points you choose to argue in your essay

- how you argue them
- the significance that you give to each point
- the evidence that you choose in support of your points
- the limitations you identify in the work of others
- the new connections you make between existing work
- the original way in which you come to your conclusion.

All of these demonstrate your uniqueness in your academic essay. You will argue points in a way that others do not; you will see meaning and significance in ideas or research differently from your peers. You will spot connections and implications that your peers do not, and your writing style will be uniquely you: the sentences, the words, the phrases, the ordering of ideas—all will be your style and set you apart from everyone else.

Moreover, as I said in Chapter Three, you do not need to use the first person pronoun, 'I' to express your opinion in an academic essay. You can use other words instead, which still make it clear that this is *your* view on the subject. For example, you do not need to say: 'I believe that wealth comes from the land.' Instead, you can use any of the following sentences to say the same thing in a strong, yet neutral, way:

The way you argue something—the examples you use, the emphasis you place, the connections you create—all convey your uniqueness.

- Wealth comes from the land.
- It is apparent that wealth comes from the land.
- This essay argues that wealth comes from the land.
- As this essay has shown, wealth comes from the land.
- This essay demonstrates that wealth comes from the land.
- The fact is that wealth comes from the land.
- It appears that wealth comes from the land.
- It is clear that wealth comes from the land.
- As the evidence suggests, wealth comes from the land.
- This suggests that wealth comes from the land.
- As a result, wealth comes from the land.

The Side Of The Argument That You Take

The most conclusive way to convey your opinion in an academic essay is through the side of the argument that you take, and the evidence that you assemble for that argument. I have said several times in this book: go for depth in your essay, not breadth. Argue things in an informed way. How do you do that? And how do you do it in a way that will get top marks? Let's revisit one of the sources of evidence discussed in Chapter Three (using authorities) and investigate this a bit further.

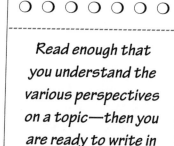

Read enough that you understand the various perspectives on a topic—then you are ready to write in support of which you think is the strongest and why.

It's All About Perspective

Often when students write an essay for their course they grab the textbook and start to write. If we were to depict this as a picture it would look a bit like the diagram below:

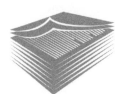

Single Perspective

They have taken material from one source of information, digested it, and written it up as an essay. Not bad, but this kind of essay will only ever get a middle grade (C or B). The reason is twofold: you have not demonstrated your ability to do research, and you only have one perspective on the topic.

Think about it for a moment. The textbook may be brilliantly written (and many are). It may even convey to you many important ideas and information written in an easy-to-understand way (again, this is useful). But it is the work of one person with a specific intention in mind—to describe the main ideas in a subject in a way that is easily understood.

Your job in an essay is to consider a topic in greater detail. To do this you need more information than your textbook can give you on this topic, AND most importantly, you need more than just the view of your textbook writer. You need to consider the views and opinions of others on the same topic. You need perspective.

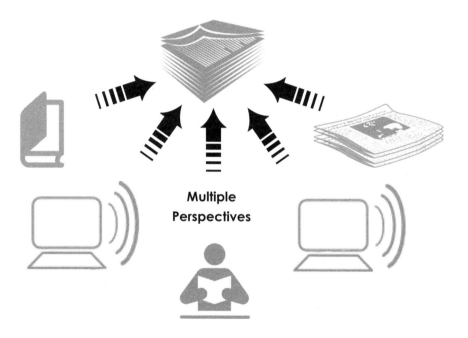

Multiple Perspectives

If I were to draw this it would look something like the diagram above. Your essay is in the middle, and you are bringing to bear on your topic a range of views and ideas coming from different perspectives. Because you have this greater variety of information you are able to write an essay that considers your topic in greater depth, and can explore the strengths or weaknesses of different viewpoints. In short, you can write a superior essay that is much better informed.

In addition, you can use the research in each of these articles or books as a source of evidence for your paragraphs. In your paragraph, you should state:

- what the person researched (including how they went about it);

- what they discovered; and
- how their discoveries or findings are relevant to your particular topic.

For example, say you were writing an essay on how creativity can be a source of new business ideas. You have found six or seven articles on the subject of creativity, and you want to use them as a source of evidence in your essay. Using a completely hypothetical example, let's say that one of the articles was written by a scholar, John Green, so here is what you might write:

Creativity has also been used to solve problems in existing organisations which has led to new business ideas. For example, Green (2006) studied 15 North American pharmaceutical firms which undertook creativity training between 1994 and 1997. Using in-depth interviews, he investigated how creativity training was used to solve problems in new product development. In 12 of the 15 firms, he found that when staff were taught brainstorming techniques their ability to solve problems increased by as much as 65 per cent. In some cases, new product development rates in these organisations were twice the industry average. Clearly, creativity training can be used as a way to increase new business ideas.

In the above paragraph I have tried to do several things. Firstly, I told you about the research. When I did this, I was specific. I told you who did it, what country it was conducted in, how many organisations were studied, in what industry, and even the time period— and I did all of this in a condensed way, trying not to waste words. Why did I do this? Because I want to make it clear to the marker that I read this research, understood it, and MOST IMPORTANTLY—this research is

Make the most of the evidence you assemble: say what is significant and how it applies to your topic.

relevant to my question and supports my case. Giving these sorts of details, I make this evident.

Secondly, in the paragraph I have told you what the person undertaking the research discovered. I have not told you ALL their discoveries, just the part that is relevant to the question that I am arguing here. Again, I used detail. You learn that problem-solving improved '65 per cent' and that in some cases it was 'twice the industry average'.

Finally, I make a connection to the essay question in the final sentence, arguing that this research makes a strong case for the use of creativity training as an aid to improved output in new product development. If I continued writing this essay, the paragraphs that followed might consider similar research in a different industry and use this to support my argument further.

Now, let's go deeper still and introduce some critical thinking—to discuss the evidence you are using in an objective way—to discern, analyse, and evaluate. Have a look at the following paragraph. I have taken Green's work on creativity as my base and instead of just presenting his work I have injected an element of critical thinking.

- -

Creativity has also been used to solve problems in existing organisations which has led to new business ideas. For example, Green (2006) studied 15 North American pharmaceutical firms which undertook creativity training between 1994 and 1997. Using in-depth interviews, he investigated how creativity training was used to solve problems in new product development. In 12 of the 15 firms, he found that when staff were taught brainstorming techniques their ability to solve problems increased by as much as 65 per cent. In some cases, new product development rates in these organisations were twice the industry average. However, while Green's research shows a link between creativity training and an increase in business ideas, it does not assess the impact that creativity training has in other industries, nor did Green account for other factors which might assist the development of creativity. For example, all the organisations that he studied

were highly profitable multinationals, which had ample
resources. What about the role of creativity in organisations
without such rich resources?

- -

Here, I have injected a critical element, by thinking more deeply
about the study that Green undertook, and looking for its strengths and
weaknesses. I have discussed two of these in my paragraph, and this
version of the paragraph will score more highly than the first version
because in this rewritten form I am showing my ability to discuss the
material in a more objective way. I am not just accepting Green's
research; I am considering its merits and its shortcomings.

Before we leave the topic of critical thinking, have a look at one
more example. Again, same topic, only this time I will add one further
element. I will inject another piece of research by someone called
Brown, to highlight either a strength or deficiency in Green's work.
Instead of me finding fault with Green's work, I let someone else's
research do it for me. The result is that my insights about this topic are
deeper still. Have a read:

- -

Creativity has also been used to solve problems within existing
organisations which has led to new business ideas. For example,
Green (2006) studied 15 North American pharmaceutical firms
which undertook creativity training between 1994 and 1997.
Using in-depth interviews, he investigated how creativity training
was used to solve problems in new product development.
In 12 of the 15 firms, he found that when staff were taught
brainstorming techniques their ability to solve problems
increased by as much as 65 per cent. In some cases, new
product development rates in these organisations were twice
the industry average. However, Green's research needs to be
read carefully. As Brown (2007) discussed in his research on
creativity in retailing firms, brainstorming may not be the only
factor. Using information from 152 retail organisations, Brown
argued that while some training was necessary, more important
was leadership style among company management. Those

organisations where leaders encouraged a creative culture (even without training) were more profitable than those that did not. Overall, while it is clear that creativity training can be beneficial for generating new ideas, it is not the only factor to be considered.

- -

So, now you have seen how it is done, go and try some critical thinking in your essay. Look for strengths in the research that you read and look for limitations. Use the material that you have to argue for the position you wish to hold in your essay. Injecting some critical thinking shows that you can stand back and look at a range of perspectives objectively. You are offering an informed and wider judgement.

Forming Your Opinion

Sometimes you will have an immediate response to what position you want to take on an essay question; whether you support a statement, or you think a particular approach is the best one. Your opinion on the matter is clear from the outset. Ironically, this is not the best way to approach an academic essay; the best approach is to read first.

Many academic essays score badly, not because the student lacked an opinion on a topic—that is generally the easy part—but because they lacked strong evidence or deeper thinking about an issue. The best counter for this difficulty is to read broadly about the topic before you commit pen to paper.

If reading terrifies you, I suggest that you do not even take notes initially. Just get two or three different sources on the topic—academic articles or books—find your favourite chair and read. Give it your full attention and let what the writers are saying fill your mind. You will encounter issues or thoughts that did not occur to you previously, and you will

Settle down in your favourite chair and read. Immerse yourself in the ideas.

begin to form a wider impression of the boundaries of the question. You will start to recognise the key areas that writers habitually mention in a topic. This is important, as it suggests to you the areas that your essay must address.

As you read more about a topic, your own opinion on that topic will galvanise in your mind. You will absorb the claims and assertions that others have put forward, and your thinking will respond to this information. In short, based on a variety of fresh information, you will come to your own opinion (or position) on a subject.

Of course, you may find that what you think at this point is exactly the same opinion that you held at the outset. That's fine. But remember, you are now in a wholly different position from which to argue your position. You have a greater range of evidence at your disposal to support your position in a way that you did not previously, and this is important. Your essay will be stronger and more convincing as a result.

On Reading

With so many demands on your time, you will need to develop a strategy for reading. If you are someone who struggles to read, just doing more of it will help. You will improve your retention and your speed through practice. But this is often not enough. You also need some other strategies if you are going to survive study and enjoy it.

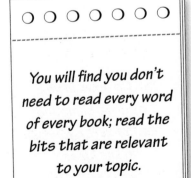

You will find you don't need to read every word of every book; read the bits that are relevant to your topic.

Attend A Speed Reading Course

Early on in my academic life I attended a speed reading course and it has proved a life saver. While not anywhere near as fast as a highly trained speed reader, I managed to improve my reading speed and learned how to rapidly scan a page, seeing if anything in particular was relevant to my essay question. If you get the opportunity to go on such a course, take it. You might not get to the place where you read four or five pages a minute—I never did—but you will increase your reading speed and your comprehension.

Head For The Index

I don't know why, but we often forget that indexes exist. They are great time savers. Book titles alone can be deceptive; get into the habit of flicking to the index in a book and seeing how many (or how few) pages have been devoted to the topic that you are studying for your essay.

Go For Articles Not Books

It is a common problem in university study: the lecturer assigns an essay topic; when you have a spare moment, you assemble a list of books that sound perfect for your essay and head for the library. But after 10 minutes of searching you arrive at the shelf to discover that someone else has got there first—where your 'golden book' should have been sitting is just empty space. Dejected, you think that your essay will never be as good as if you had that one special book.

You are wrong. Actually, the reverseis true. The student who staggered out of the library holding a stack of 15 books on the essay topic is not demonstrating anything more than their ability to find books on a shelf. They will never have the time to read all of those books. Chances are, they will read little more than the first one on their pile.

The big deception is that books are the primary way to get information for academic essays. In most cases they are not. An important way scholars communicate their ideas is not through books, it is through articles.

In 30 minutes of careful searching using a library database, you can locate sufficient articles to write a solid essay.

So the best way to arm yourself for writing an academic essay, and the fastest route to quickly grasping the areas of debate or interest in an area, is to assemble a set of articles. It is also the smartest survival strategy for life at college or university.

Which would you rather do: read six books on one subject (at 350 pages per book), or six articles, with an average length of 15 pages each? It doesn't take a genius to realise that the second approach works best, and in this age of databases and search engines you can easily find six to ten articles on your topic in half an hour or so. Take them away, sit down, and read what people are saying on your topic. There are two types of articles you need to be aware of:

1. Articles In Newspapers And Magazines

You may find articles in newspapers on your essay topic and they can be useful. More frequently, you will find articles in popular magazines or quarterlies in your subject area that are aimed at the professional reader. For example, they might be magazines targeted at health professionals, or publications for teachers, dentists, businesspeople, entrepreneurs, or social workers. Whatever it is, these sorts of publications can yield some useful information, especially case examples of organisations or individuals that might be related to your essay topic.

2. Scholarly Journals

These are published by academic publishing houses with articles based on research done by qualified people in the field. Every discipline has them: psychology, art history, science, medicine, business, English, architecture. They are research based and peer reviewed, which means that before anyone's work is published, a group of other scholars have looked over the article and decided whether it was worthy of publication. Was it credible, rigorous, useful, and thorough?

In most cases, these are an excellent source of information for your essay. They are not the only source (as the sources mentioned in Chapter Three suggested), but they are useful as the information presented in them can be taken as credible. I say 'credible' meaning that the information is based on investigation and research.

However, you need to read your articles carefully. Just like many things, you will find that scholars also hold divergent views on a topic, and in these journals they argue their position based on the evidence they have assembled. You will find people arguing both for your viewpoint on a topic, as well as those offering counter-arguments. For you, about to write an essay, both are useful as you begin to understand the range of perspectives on a topic and its key points.

Let Someone Else Do The Hard Work

The other big plus with scholarly articles is the reference list at the end of the article. All the material that the author has cited or referenced in his or her article is listed alphabetically. Your original problem was finding relevant material for your question. Here, someone who knows this subject in depth has already done the hard work for you. Scan the entries in the reference list and highlight those that look relevant to your essay topic.

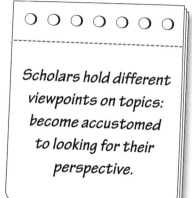

Scholars hold different viewpoints on topics: become accustomed to looking for their perspective.

Next, use a search engine or a library catalogue to find the author on the reference list whose article seems to be related to your question, and then look at the reference list at the end of *their* article. In snowball fashion, within a very short time, you can have a solid stack of material, all written by authorities in your area of study, and all exactly on the topic of your essay. Will you now run out of things to say in your essay? Never.

How To Use Quotes

Quotes can be a useful source of evidence for an essay. Often, you are looking at a book or article while you are writing your essay and you notice that someone has summed up what you wanted to say just brilliantly. Carefully, you type it out at the appropriate place in your essay:

> *'Good writers take care to pick the right word.'*

> Professor Charles Penhandy (2006, p. 5)

Pleased with your find, you move on to the next idea you want to discuss in your essay. Wrong! That is not the right way to use a quote, and you will not gain marks—in fact, you will probably lose them. When you use a quote you must demonstrate your understanding of how that quote relates to the topic at hand. Do not assume that your marker will read the quote the same way you do, or comprehend its relevance to your argument. It is your job as the writer of the essay to make this connection clear in the sentences that follow the use of a quote. Let me demonstrate with the following:

Writing is not a difficult activity but it does take practice and a knowledge of some of the basic rules of sentence construction and style. One of the typical mistakes that many people make when writing is to use the first word that comes to their mind. This is an error. As Professor Charles Penhandy remarks: 'Good writers take care to pick the right word.' (Penhandy, 2006, p. 5) Penhandy's argument is that good writing displays clarity and precision. He claims that this does not happen immediately when we write. Instead, clarity emerges through careful selection of the right word to convey a thought.

Can you see the difference? I might have inserted this quote from Professor Penhandy, and then hurried on to my next point in the essay. But if I had, I would have lost any chance of gaining marks as I would not have demonstrated understanding.

Your job is to show that you understand the material at hand, and you do this by applying it in a way that makes sense. You can even restate the quote in your own words. Saying something like: 'What Penhandy seems to be suggesting here is that...' (Now continue the sentence with your interpretation.)

This approach is quite acceptable in an academic essay. It shows the marker that you have thought about the material you are working with in a deeper way, and not just thrown in a quote for effect.

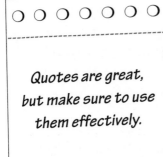

Quotes are great, but make sure to use them effectively.

The One Idea

The final point about style and your essay is to do with how many ideas you write about. It is easy to fall into the trap of trying to cram too many ideas into one paragraph. On average, a paragraph is about seven to eight sentences, and is approximately 140–160 words long. This is enough space to develop one idea well. It is not, though, enough space to cover dog breeding, the importance of dog training, and to tell me about the most popular dog name—which, apparently, is Max—all in one blinding, fact-stuffed paragraph. In fact, when you put more than one idea in a paragraph it usually shows that you do not have enough information on your ideas to develop them further.

If you adhere to the sorts of planning tools described in Chapter Two, then you will already be starting to give some thought to how your essay should be structured. You will have listed the key points (depending on the length of your essay) that you wish to cover. Now is the time for discipline. When you write the essay, stick to the framework you have developed. Write the paragraph on the idea that you said you would. Don't let yourself be lured down enticing side alleys. If you have some new inspiration and it is worthy, then give it the space it deserves and write a further paragraph about this additional development.

If you have another idea that warrants discussion, write another paragraph, and develop it fully.

If you get comments in the margin of your work from the marker—such as 'expand', or 'superficial', or 'too general'—this is your cue that you need to develop the main idea of your paragraph more fully, before going on to the next point. Likely, you are hitting the reader with too big a spread of information and not enough depth.

Delve deeper into the examples that you use and show their relevance to your work. Draw out a pertinent illustration and discuss its strengths and weaknesses. Consider a relevant quote from both the positive and negative side. Explore the subtlety of a particular point. Force yourself to think more deeply and start to write that way: you will write a more impressive, and higher-scoring, essay as a result. Instead of comments like 'too brief' or 'rushed' in the margin, you will start to see comments like 'well developed', 'thoughtful', 'good insight'.

CHAPTER SEVEN

Referencing And Other Chores

Academic essays require that you reference your work. That is, identify in some form the source of the ideas that you discuss. Not all you write comes out of your own head; when the material you are writing is based on something that someone else has written, or facts or information you found somewhere else, you must acknowledge this in your essay in the form of a reference.

Always refer to your institution's specific referencing guidelines to ensure you meet the expectations relevant to your course.

Not to do this is what academics call 'plagiarism'. In short, intellectual stealing—passing off ideas that someone else had, or work that others have done, as your own. The penalties for plagiarism are usually severe, and can include being thrown out of your course of study. So do not do it, either consciously or unconsciously. You can avoid it completely if you reference.

Referencing is not hard. The basic rule of thumb is that if you have written a paragraph or a sentence, and you found the information in that sentence somewhere else, then you must acknowledge this with a reference. The question then is: What sort of reference?

Two Types Of Referencing

There are two main types of referencing systems: the author/date system and the footnote/endnote system. In different universities and different subject areas preferences have arisen for one particular system over the other, so find out which is acceptable in your course. The important thing to remember is that they all achieve the same thing, which is to provide you with a way of acknowledging the source of your ideas and information.

Most courses will inform you at the start which referencing system they want you to use in your essay and many courses will give you a detailed guide to some of the basic ways to reference material from books, articles, the internet, etc. What I want to do here is outline briefly for you the main differences between the two referencing systems and, more importantly, give you some ways to write sentences using references so that you become better at it, and more relaxed using reference material. In the sections that follow, we are first going to consider the author/date system and the conventions it adopts for referencing, and then briefly the footnote/endnote system.

Author/Date

Author/date is an in-text referencing system, which means that you reference the ideas within the text of the paragraph or sentence that you are writing. It is called author/date as this refers to the order in which you acknowledge the source of the idea. So, every time you discuss the ideas of a particular person, or have used facts or evidence from some outside source, you acknowledge the author and the date thus (Smith, 2007).

Simple! What this reference is saying is that I have read the work of Smith, and am discussing some of his or her ideas in my paragraph. The year following Smith's name is the year of publication of his or her work. Often, you will find a reference like this placed at the conclusion of a sentence before the full stop (Smith, 2007). Never use the first name and surname. It is ALWAYS the surname. Now let's look at a few handy variations on this convention.

Working With The Author/Date System In Your Paragraphs

If the particular article that you were using had two authors, then the reference in your text would look like this (Walker & Jones, 2006). Or, if you wanted to say it more directly, you could state: 'Walker and Jones (2006) are quite particular in their writing on this topic.' Whether Walker and Jones had written a book or an article is not known from the in-text reference. If you want to know this information, you need to look in the reference list at the back of the essay.

In practice, the author/date system is exactly as it says: the author's surname, followed by the date of publication.

Let's look at a few more author variations before we consider this system in more detail. Say, for example, you had a piece of research that had three authors. It does not matter whether it is a book, an article, a government report, or a chapter in a book, in-text referencing does not make this distinction in the body of the essay. Merely, it would show it thus (Jones, Brown & Wallingham, 1998). If you use this same piece of research later in your essay, you do not specify all three authors again. Instead, you use the Latin abbreviation 'et al.', which translates, 'and everyone'. So the second time I mention my prior article it would be (Jones et al., 1998).

There are two more useful twists to be aware of. First, if you want to refer to several studies or pieces of research at the same time, then you can do this by separating them with a semi-colon (Jones et al., 1998; Harbunkle, 2001; Thompson, 2007). Second, if a particular piece of highly useful information came from the internet, I would include in my text a reference to this, giving the URL (http://www.apastyle.apa.org).

Direct Quotes

All that I have said so far assumes that the material that you have discussed was not a direct quote—that is, you have not used word for word what any of these authors wrote. If you want to use a direct quote in your paragraph you need to do a fuller reference.

Say, for example, you wanted to use a quote from Smith that said: 'Monday was never a good day at the office.' Then you need to add one more detail to your reference and that is the page number on which the quote can be found. So you would write:

> *As Smith remarked: 'Monday was never a good day at the office'*
> *(Smith, 2007, p. 5).*

It is essential that you give this fuller reference EVERY time that you quote a piece of work directly. Not to do so may result in you getting zero for your essay grade, as most markers will assume that you are passing off material that you found elsewhere as your own, hiding the fact that someone else actually wrote it.

Don't give a direct quote expecting your marker to see what you see: tell them why it is relevant to your essay.

The test: if someone can find exactly what you have written somewhere else, then that is a direct quote. If what you have written so closely resembles, for example, Smith's work that you have just changed a couple of words, then you are still copying. It is not Smith's exact words, but they are so close that you will be judged to be passing off Smith's work as your own.

If all this leaves you concerned about how on earth you might get close to Smith's work without getting into trouble, read on. It is easy to avoid plagiarism.

Using Author/Date References With Confidence

If you want to talk generally about someone's ideas—for example, you would like to write a paragraph describing the importance of Smith's ideas, or a particular discovery that he made—you would have to reference this. There are several accepted conventions that you can use. Each offers a slightly different alternative in terms of writing style. Consider the following.

Firstly, you can reference Smith at the start of the first sentence when you are about to talk about his ideas. It is generally accepted that this reference covers your continued discussion of Smith's ideas for the rest of the paragraph, so further references to the same person within that paragraph are unnecessary. It looks like this:

Many writers have investigated the importance of honesty. Smith (2007), for example, explored honesty among the lost tribes of South America. He found that 90 per cent of the tribespeople were honest and this was largely due to their upbringing. Family values and loyalty were important and these were communicated to children from an early stage in their life.

Alternatively, you can place the reference at the end of the sentence, allowing you to write slightly differently. Again, this is perfectly acceptable; which one you choose is up to you and how you want the sentence to read.

Many writers have investigated the importance of honesty. Smith, for example, explored honesty among the lost tribes of South America (Smith, 2007). He found that 90 per cent of the tribespeople were honest and this was largely due to their upbringing. Family values and loyalty were important and these were communicated to children from an early stage in their life.

Of course, if I was offering a direct quote of Smith in the paragraph, I would have to write it like this:

Many writers have investigated the importance of honesty. Smith, for example, explored honesty among the lost tribes of South America: 'Nearly all the people were honest. I could not believe it' (Smith, 2007, p. 7). He found that 90 per cent of the tribespeople were honest and this was largely due to their upbringing. Family values and loyalty were important and these were communicated to children from an early stage in their life.

- -

Creating A Reference List Using Author/Date

At the conclusion of your essay you need to create a reference list or bibliography. This is where you list in alphabetical order (by author's surname) all the works that you have referred to in the body of your essay. Anything that you referenced in your essay must be listed here.

The conventions for listing books, articles, newspaper articles, and internet sites differ at times according to what subject you are studying and the preferences of your discipline. However, the APA system, which is one of the author/date referencing systems, is commonplace today, and so I will offer some frequent examples of this below. APA stands for American Psychological Association; it is their system.

Following are some of the more common occurrences which students have to refer to in their essays and how to reference them in your bibliography (or reference list).

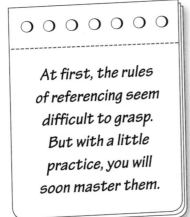

At first, the rules of referencing seem difficult to grasp. But with a little practice, you will soon master them.

Journal Article: Single Author

If you used an article written by a single author, Vernon Smith, then you would reference it thus in your reference list:

Smith, V. B. (2006). Classic adventures in epic poetry. *Poetry Today*, *45*(6), 123–129.

- The numbers 45(6) refer to the volume number of the journal (which here is 45) and the issue number of the journal (which is 6). The year in brackets (2006) is the copyright year of the journal. Note the single space between the initials of Smith's two first names, and the spacing and use of commas or periods between the other elements of the reference. You need to conform to this format.

- Also, the convention is to italicise the title of the journal, and the volume number of the publication from which the article came. Everything else in the reference is in plain (or roman) text.
- And even though I knew Smith's first name, I did not use it. The convention with APA style is to use the author's initials, NOT their first name. This is the rule—stick to it.
- Finally, in the titles of books or articles the convention is to capitalise the first letter of the title, and leave the remaining words in lower case. Unless one of the words in the title is a proper name—watch for this.

Journal Article: Two Authors

If the article had been written by two people, Vernon Smith and Elizabeth Brown, then the reference would be as follows:

Smith, V. & Brown, E. (2004). Renaissance poetry in France. *Poetry Today, 35*(4), 102–124.

- You will see that there are a couple of differences here. Because there is a proper name in the title—France—I have capitalised this.
- Also, when you have two authors, you do not include more than the first initial of their name. While in the first example I used both initials from the author, V. B. Smith, in this second example, where he has written the article with Elizabeth Brown, I have only used the first initial of his name.

Journal Article: Three Or More Authors

Here is a journal article with four authors:

Smith, V. B., Brown, E. J., Kennedy, S. F. W. & Eidleman, D. (1995). The geography of lower Russia. *Geographic Quarterly, 65*(1), 345–372.

- The only difference between the two-author reference and the multiple-author reference is that with three or more authors you can again use all the initials from their first names (if you have them).

Newspaper Articles

If you use a newspaper article in your essay, then you need to reference it at the end of your essay, just like anything else. The two most common forms of newspaper articles are those where you have an author and those where no author is shown. Here is how to do both:

Wigglesworth, K. T. (2004, November 12). How Britain's labour force is making the most of the summer. *Midland Times*, p. A15.

Why Britain's labour force is taking more time for holidays. (2003, July 14). *Midland Times*, pp. 16–17.

There are a couple of things that are being added here that you did not do with journal articles.
- Firstly, you are giving the month and date of the newspaper article.
- Secondly, you are using 'p.' as an abbreviation for page, and showing the page number of the newspaper article (including the section, if applicable) at the end of your reference.
- Thirdly, if the article goes across two or more pages, then 'pp.' is used to indicate the range of pages.

Referencing Books And Other Sources Using Author/Date System

Books adopt many of the same conventions as outlined above. However, instead of using volume numbers and issue numbers as you did for journal articles, you are going to show the place of publication of the book (the city where the publisher is situated) and the name of the publisher.

Again, as in referencing journal articles, you only use the author's initials, and not their full first name. Some books go to more than one edition; you need to show this in your reference.

There follows two examples: one for a single-author book in its first edition, and the other for the same single-author book in its fifth edition, 20 years later.

Book: One Author

Cowley, C. D. (1978). *Mastering the art of painting: English artists speak about their work*. London: Collins.

Cowley, C. D. (1998). *Mastering the art of painting: English artists speak about their work* (5th ed.). London: Collins.

Book: Two Authors

Cowley, C. D. & Higgins, G. F. W. (1987). *Painting when the sea no longer calls: A guide to painting for retired Australian fishermen*. New York: Harper.

- With books (where you have two authors) use middle initials of their names if you have them. In addition, for all three of the above examples I have shown you how to deal with a title that has a main title followed by a subtitle. The rule is simple: Capitalise the first letter after the colon, and any other proper noun in the title. So, for the final example shown above, the 'A' after the colon was capitalised, as was 'Australian'.

Book: Three Or More Authors

Cowley, C. D., Higgins, G. F. W., MacMillan, J. & Hepburn, I. (1987). *The lost tourist: A guide to great Italian mazes*. London: Harper.

Book: With An Editor Not An Author

Bright, J. F. (Ed.). (1967). *Smart solutions for smart mathematicians*. New York: Viking.

- If you have a book that is an edited collection of chapters, so the person whose name on the front cover is shown as the editor of the book, not the writer, then you can reference it as above. Here, the abbreviation 'Ed.' stands for editor.

- If you want to reference a particular chapter in the book, the example shown below illustrates how to do this. This example is of a book that has two editors, so you can see how this is accomplished. Note, there are a couple of additions to style here: firstly, the chapter is given; secondly, 'Eds.' is the abbreviation for editors; and thirdly, the pages of the particular chapter are also given.

Macefield, H. D. (1995). Knowing right from wrong. In J. F. Bright & J. W. Smart (Eds.), *Moral dilemmas in statistics* (pp. 314–339). New York: Viking.

Book: With No Editor Or Author

How can there be a book with no author or editor? It actually happens more often than you think. Publishing firms put out books—even dictionaries—without an obvious editor or author. The publisher itself has commissioned someone to work on the project, with their own company being the 'brand', or the apparent author, of the book. Study guides can be like this, as can travel guides, encyclopaedias, and other reference works. Here is how you deal with this sort of publication in your reference list:

Ocean View Books. (2007). *Beaches of the South Pacific* (2nd ed.). Melbourne: Author.

Points to note:

- Firstly, the use of the publisher in place of the author's surname at the start of the reference—this is the convention.
- Secondly, the use of the word 'Author' at the end of the reference. This is done to indicate that the author of the work is the publisher shown at the outset of the reference.

Thesis

If you have found information from a thesis, either a master's thesis or a Ph.D. thesis, this is how you can reference these in your bibliography:

McCarthy, S. (2003). Singers from the sixties: An analysis of the place and role of fashion in the music industry. Unpublished master's thesis, University of Sydney, Sydney, Australia.

Warren, F. W. (2006). Psychological testing: The case for random testing of shop employees. Unpublished doctoral dissertation, University of Nottingham, Nottingham, England.

Interview

Some information you obtain may be from a personal interview. You do not include this information in your reference list, but instead cite it in-text—that is, during the paragraph of your essay in which it is used. Here is the convention:

> *'If education is going to make an impact, some teachers better start performing more highly than they are at present'*
> (J. Micklehorn, personal communication, 15 December, 2007).

Internet Referencing

With the increased use of the internet, students often ask how to reference material sourced from the internet. Using the APA author/date system, here are three of the more common instances: an article in an internet-only journal; an internet source for a printed article; and information retrieved from a company website.

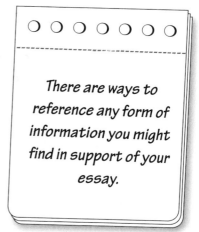

There are ways to reference any form of information you might find in support of your essay.

If your article is ONLY available from an electronic journal, use the following:

Berkins, P. W. (2005, August 15). Flying for beginners. *Flyers Monthly*, 7, Article 7374c. Retrieved March 22, 2007, from http://www.flyersmonthly.com/volume7/374c.html

- Note: your reference should include the date of retrieval, and the URL to link directly with the article. The first name in the reference is the surname of the author.

If you have found an article on the internet that is also available in print form—that is, the electronic version is just the online-stored version, then you do not need to make any reference to its URL or retrieval date, but you insert the words '[Electronic Version]' after the article title as follows:

> Hapworth, S. W. (2007). Twelve ways to increase your income [Electronic Version]. *Executive Wealth*, 5, 33–37.

However, if the electronic version of the article is only based on the printed version, and is not EXACTLY the same, then you need to reference it thus:

> Hapworth, S. W. (2007). Twelve ways to increase your income. *Executive Wealth*, 5, 33–37. Retrieved September 22, 2007, from http://www.executivewealth.com/volume5/228a.html

Finally, if you have found information from some company documents on a website, or a private organisation, and you want to include it in your essay with the appropriate reference, this is how you show this in the reference list. For this information, I have assumed that there is no date showing on the web document. This is indicated by the abbreviation '(n.d.)'.

> Singapore Business Investment Association. (n.d.). *Quick survey of investment opportunities in Singapore.* Retrieved June 22, 2005, from http://www.singaporebusinessinvest.com/surveys/216. html

Footnote/Endnote System

The main alternative to the author/date system is the footnote/endnote system. Frequently, the footnote/endnote system is used in history, literature, and the arts. It provides more detailed reporting than the author/date system, as it allows the writer to add comments within the footnote or endnote to supplement the main text. These might be small discussions of the sources used, or directions to alternative sources of information on the topic. Moreover, footnotes/endnotes allow the writer to keep the text free of references in cumbersome brackets, which permits greater fluidity in the writing style.

Both footnotes and endnotes use a reference marker which is placed at the end of a sentence. This can be symbols († * #) or, more frequently, consecutive numbers (1, 2, 3, 4 . . . i, ii, iii, iv . . .). For example, if you have just referred to a particular fact or piece of evidence, you insert a numbered reference marker at the end of the sentence like this.1

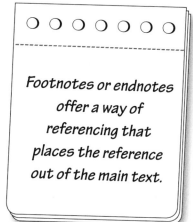

Footnotes or endnotes offer a way of referencing that places the reference out of the main text.

If you are using footnotes at the bottom of the page a corresponding identical number appears where you can type in the reference to the work you have used. If you are using endnotes, again the identical number appears, only this time at the end of the document. For a single-author book, my footnote (or endnote) would take the following form:

> 1. John A. Provost, *The Literature of the East Indies* (Washington: Collins Press, 1996): 22–27.

At the conclusion of my work would be a bibliography which would list in alphabetical order (by author's surname) all the sources referenced in my essay.

A convention in footnote/endnote systems is that the first time a work is referenced the full reference for the work is given. For successive references from the same work, you can use a shortened form of the initial reference. This helps speed up the writing process and eliminates unnecessary repetition. The short-form reference will include the author's surname, the main title of the work (in abbreviated form), and the respective page reference. For example, if I were to include a short-form reference for the example shown above I would type:

> 2. Provost, *East Indies*, 43.

Like author/date systems, footnote/endnote systems have rules for documenting single authors, multiple authors, editors, reports, electronic references, and any other possible permutation you care to consider. I am only going to list a few of the more frequent here. If you want more information, one of the best guides is The Chicago Manual of Style which is published by The University of Chicago Press. It is an invaluable reference work and most public libraries or university libraries will have a copy.

Here are a few examples of footnote/endnote references: one using a journal article, a second using an edited book, and a third using a book with two authors. For each, I have first listed their initial reference in the text. Following this is the short-form reference you would use if you were to mention the same work a second time in the essay.

Note that unlike the author/date system, in footnotes and endnotes all the words in the book, or article, title are capitalised except small words, such as of, from, to, as, in, and, etc. and articles, such as a, the. Also, the author's full first name is given, if you have this information.

3. Wally B. Davidson, 'I Believe in the Power of the Pen', *Writing Quarterly* 22, no. 3 (2005): 161–62.

4. John Filemore, 'The Rights and Duties of Management', in *Management: The Big Picture*, ed. H. F. Grouber (New York: Chronicle Press, 1995): 22.

5. Sharon Jackson and Matilda Pettigrew, *England's Kings and their Interesting Habits* (Cambridge, MA: Gora Books, 1986).

6. Davidson, 'Power of the Pen': 177.

7. Filemore, 'Rights and Duties: 127, 134.

8. Jackson and Pettigrew, *England's Kings*: 39.

For both author/date and footnote/endnote systems you assemble a reference list (or bibliography) showing all your sources at the end of your essay.

As with all referencing systems, you must list all the works you have used in your essay in the bibliography (or reference list) at the conclusion of your work. With footnotes/endnotes a few stylistic differences apply. Firstly, whereas the footnote used in the essay commenced with the author's first name, in the bibliography the authors are listed by surname.

Referencing allows you to support your evidence in a credible and rigorous way.

Secondly, whereas footnotes in the essay used commas to separate the various parts of the reference, in the bibliography this is replaced with the period. Note too, brackets are removed from book entries. Furthermore, in the bibliography, page references are for whole chapters, or for the whole article, never for the individual pages referred to in the essay.

Using the same examples as above, here is how they would appear in the bibliography at the end of my essay:

Davidson, Wally B. 'I Believe in the Power of the Pen.' *Writing Quarterly* 22, no. 3 (2005): 150–178.

Filemore, John. 'The Rights and Duties of Management.' In *Management: The Big Picture*, edited by H. F. Grouber: 15–35. New York: Chronicle Press, 1995.

Jackson, Sharon and Matilda Pettigrew. *England's Kings and their Interesting Habits*. Cambridge, MA: Gora Books, 1986.

Both the author/date and footnote/endnote referencing systems have much to recommend them. Each allows you as the writer to discuss ideas in a more robust manner than if you had no such system, and provide the reader with a way to consider your points and arguments in more depth by looking back into the sources which have formed the basis of your discussion.

For More Help

If the information or type of reference you must document is not covered here, or if you want more detailed information on referencing, I recommend the following:

American Psychological Association. (2001). *Publication manual of the American Psychological Association* (5th ed.). Washington: Author.

University of Chicago Press. (1982). *The Chicago manual of style: The essential guide for writers, editors, and publishers* (15th ed.). Chicago: Author.

Amato, C. (1995). *The world's easiest guide to using the APA: A user-friendly manual for formatting research papers according to the American Psychological Association style guide* (3rd ed.). Corona, CA: Stargazer.

To find out more about author/date referencing systems online, try: http://www.apastyle.apa.org

To find out more about Chicago Manual of Style online, try: http://www.chicagomanualofstyle.org

Referencing: Don't Forget Why

As a final note on referencing I would say: Remember why you are doing it. You are writing an essay that has used evidence from sources outside of your immediate knowledge. This information you acknowledge in your essay in the form of a reference. But do not make the mistake of thinking that the more references you cram into your text, the higher the grade you will receive. This is missing the purpose.

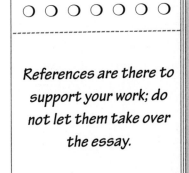

References are there to support your work; do not let them take over the essay.

Terrifyingly, some students present essays that have a reference almost at the end of every sentence. They might think they are dazzling their marker with their abundance of sources; they are not. This is poor work that is displaying a lack of knowledge, not superiority of insight.

In these situations, two questions are going through the marker's mind. Firstly: Where is the depth in this essay that is going over so much information so quickly? Secondly: Where is the originality?

If sentence after sentence comes from somewhere else and is describing someone else's work, then where are your own thoughts, analysis, propositions, discussion, examination, and summation? They must be there, or all that you are doing in your essay is repeating the ideas of others. That will not score well—indeed, it will likely fail.

How you demonstrate understanding in an essay is to show that you have assembled relevant material, you have clearly understood what this material is about, you have applied it correctly to support your point, and using this material, you have come to well-supported conclusions. Just describing the work of others in your essay and including copious references merely demonstrates that you can go to the library and find some books on your topic. It does not demonstrate understanding or insight.

CHAPTER EIGHT

Essay Writing For Exams

Essays remain one of the most popular choices for assessing your ability in a subject. Every year, at the end of semester, or at the end of term, the onslaught begins—and essays are everywhere! Even in classes where the subject is intensely practical, the essay is often used as an assessment tool for the final exam. Some people dread this. They only need to hear the word 'essay' mentioned and they begin to think about taking another subject.

You need to approach writing for an exam slightly differently than writing for your course during the year.

You do not need to worry. There are some basic things that distinguish essays that do well in final exams from those that do not. If you learn these techniques and invest some time in practising them before your examinations, you will quickly see that exam essays are not as bad as you thought.

You will write your essays with renewed confidence and greater skill. Your essays will be stronger and more direct, and you will find that your writing speed increases, allowing you more time to compose an outstanding answer. Getting better grades for exam essays is well within your grasp.

Differences And Similarities Between Exam Essays And Course Essays

In style, there are many similarities between the essay you write during course time and the one you would write in a final examination. However, this said, exam conditions are more pressured, and as a result, you need to approach your essay for an exam in a slightly different manner. The biggest change is the amount of time you have to prepare your essay, order your thoughts, and then get them down on paper. Often, you only have 45 minutes or an hour per essay. Consequently, from the outset you need to modify your approach to the plan.

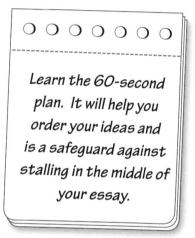

Learn the 60-second plan. It will help you order your ideas and is a safeguard against stalling in the middle of your essay.

Quick Plans

For an examination essay you must plan. As an examiner it is very easy to distinguish between those essays that followed a plan and those that did not. Those that did are nearly always in the top half of the class. If you plan, you will know what you want to say, you will have established an order to your thoughts, and you will never suffer that awful moment midstream in an examination essay when you realise that you have forgotten what you were going to say next. With a plan by your side, you merely refresh your memory and continue to write.

But how do you plan effectively in such a short space of time? Simple. You brainstorm, then prioritise. I call it the 60-second plan. Literally, this is all it takes.

There are two easy steps:

Step 1

Brainstorm. Jot down any key ideas or thoughts that come to mind in regard to the topic you have to write your essay on. Write these words in list form, and keep each entry to no longer than three words. Speed and simplicity are the aims. Each of the words you write down should be just sufficient to act as a prompt to your brain when it comes time to write.

Step 2

Prioritise. Look at your list and write a number down by each point. The numbers are the order in which you will discuss these points in your essay. So, 1 would be the first paragraph (or idea for discussion), 2 the next paragraph, and so on. Within 60 seconds you have a quick sketch plan on a piece of paper that has allowed you to both recall the information you know on a topic, as well as order it in a logical way ready to write an exam essay. You will now produce a stronger and more confident answer as a result.

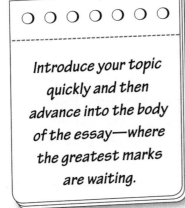

Introduce your topic quickly and then advance into the body of the essay—where the greatest marks are waiting.

Lightning Introductions

A critical difference between the essay you might write in your course and the essay you write for an examination is the introduction. You do not have time to write a lengthy one- or two-paragraph introduction. More to the point, if you did, you would not get any marks for it.

The marks for an examination essay are sitting in the body of the essay where you give your points and make your arguments. What you say in your introduction is merely getting you there as quickly as possible. In an examination setting, allow yourself two or three sentences (at most) for your introduction. Any more than this is wasting time.

For your introductory sentences do not try and be fancy. Be direct, and use key words or phrases from the question set in the examination paper without writing the question out in full. Then, in your next sentence, declare your argument explicitly so there is no confusion about what you intend to say in your essay. For example, if your examination question was something like:

'Money is the root of all evil.' Discuss.

For your lightning introduction, you could write:

- -

This essay will examine the statement that money is the root of all evil. In particular, this essay will argue that money alone has no moral qualities—instead, it is the greed, avarice, and materialism that results from the unconstrained pursuit of money that gives money its negative attributes. Ultimately, it is how the user treats money, not money itself, which is the deciding factor.

- -

And off I go. Even from this very short introduction, you would expect the first section of my essay to be arguing that money has no moral qualities and the following sections to consider greed, avarice, and materialism respectively. In addition, the marker is left in no doubt over the intent and argument of my essay.

How Much Should You Write?

Before I say anything about this topic, there is something that you must realise: someone might write three pages on a topic in an examination essay and score full marks; equally, a different person might write double this on the same topic and also score full marks; and I have seen essays that were six pages long that failed to pass.

What's going on? The problem is not the length of your essay, but focus. A superior essay addresses the topic quickly and stays on topic. There is no padding or waffle: points are clear, thoughtful, and evidenced by detailed examples. The essay is clearly structured, with each part of the question answered. You can do this in three pages, and do it brilliantly; you can do this in six pages, and do it brilliantly. Ultimately, in an exam the issue is not how much you write, but what you write.

But how much should you write? As

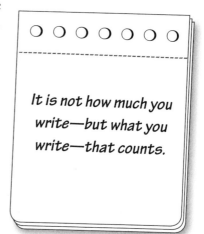

It is not how much you write—but what you write—that counts.

a rough guide, work on one side of an A4 page per 15 minutes allocated for the essay, writing on each line in an answer booklet. So, if your examination is three hours long, and you have to write three essays, then the average length of the essays written in the exam will be about four A4 sides per essay. There will be people who write double that. They are very fast writers who can get their thoughts down in rapid fashion. Don't be put off by this. As I said, length does not always correspond to higher grades.

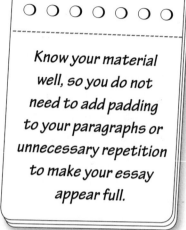

Know your material well, so you do not need to add padding to your paragraphs or unnecessary repetition to make your essay appear full.

As an examiner, you can be reading arduously through someone's eight-page essay waiting hopefully for them to get round to answering the question that was asked. It is distressing to see so much writing put in for so few marks, but it happens. How do you avoid that? Here are some suggestions.

Detail And General

Marks in your examination essay are won in the detail. Do not make generalised statements. Be specific, and back up your specific points with detailed examples.

- *Don't say:* There were many casualties during the Franco-Prussian War.
- *Say:* Sixty-five thousand soldiers died during the Franco-Prussian War of 1870–1871.
- *Don't say:* The United States economy boomed in the 1990s and manufacturing was profitable.
- *Say:* The United States economy grew on average 4 per cent a year between 1990 and 2000, topping the list of OECD nations. Manufacturing contributed 60 per cent of this economic growth.
- *Don't say:* Leonardo da Vinci was a highly creative Renaissance painter who gave us many masterpieces.

- **Say:** Leonardo da Vinci (1452–1519) was a highly creative Renaissance painter who gave us many masterpieces, including the *Mona Lisa*, *The Last Supper*, and *The Return of the Magi*.

In all these examples, the first sentence says something interesting but does not give enough detail to score a mark because it demonstrates no knowledge. The second sentence opens the way for a mark because it uses detail. It is precise, it is specific, and it displays the writer's knowledge of the topic.

Do not make sweeping, generalised statements in your sentences thinking that you will score marks. You will not. Your examination is meant to demonstrate your knowledge. So demonstrate it: be specific in what you write in your sentences.

Using Sub-Headings

One of the problems any examination marker faces is recognising when you have changed direction in an essay, or are emphasising a new point. To remedy this, I recommend using sub-headings in your examination, just like those used in this book, to introduce longer sections in your examination essay. For example, you might have a sub-heading introducing a section that contains three or four paragraphs discussing a particular topic or central idea in your essay.

How many sub-headings would you use in an exam essay? Well, as a rough guide, I would suggest that you think in terms of three to four sub-headings per essay in your exam. That is enough.

The benefit is that as an examiner, each time you see a sub-heading it is a clue to what the next section is going to be about, and you mentally prepare yourself knowing that the previous section is over and a new section of the essay is about to begin.

This is doubly important in an essay written under exam conditions. You want to make it absolutely clear when you are talking about a particular idea, and when you change topic and begin discussing a different idea. Sub-headings are a foolproof indicator. Also, they are a helpful prompt to check if you have covered all the points in the essay that you said in your introduction you were going to cover. In less than a minute you can flick back through several pages of text and eye up the sub-headings.

Using Space To Your Advantage

Seeing a full page of text—line after line of writing—pushed out to the margins of the page, with no paragraphs anywhere in sight, is

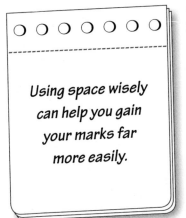

Using space wisely can help you gain your marks far more easily.

an examiner's nightmare. The irony is that even when you tell a hundred students not to do it, and explain a better approach to setting out their exam answers, around 5 per cent will ignore your recommendations. Do not be one of these people. Take a hint. Looking at a full page of text with no obvious paragraphs is distressing. As an examiner you instantly think: How will I know when this person finishes discussing one idea in the essay and moves on to the next? How will I understand how the argument in their essay develops?

'That's easy,' you say. 'You will read my entire essay.' And of course, the examiner will. But I challenge you. Write out a page of text with no breaks, very little space in the margins, and with no paragraphs, just line after line. Then read it 199 times over. Are you feeling refreshed and alert and ready to comprehend the arguments in the paper the 200th time you pick it up? Because that is what your examiner is facing. They might have marked 199 exams before they finally hold your examination paper in their hands.

At this point, you want to make your exam stand out. You want to make it easy for the examiner to understand what you have written, and you want to make it especially easy for them to give you marks. Use space to your advantage. Use sub-headings as I suggest above. In addition, begin leaving a single line space between paragraphs in your examination essay. Write a paragraph of text—six or seven sentences line after line—then, when you complete your paragraph, skip a line on the examination book before you start your next paragraph.

Exam Essay A

One of the problems any examination marker faces is how to know easily when you have changed direction in an essay, or are emphasising a new point. I recommend using sub-headings in your examination, just like those used in this book. Each time you see a sub-heading it is a clue to what the paragraph is about, and as an examiner you mentally prepare yourself knowing that the previous idea is over, and a new idea is about to commence. This is doubly important in an essay written under exam conditions. You want to make it absolutely clear when you are talking about a particular idea, and when you change topic, and begin discussing a different idea. Sub-headings are a foolproof indicator. Also they are a helpful prompt to you also to check if you have covered all the points in the essay that you said you were going to cover. In less than a minute you can flick back through several pages of text and eye up the sub-headings. Seeing a full page of text–line after line of writing–pushed out to the margins of the page with no paragraphs anywhere in sight is an examiner's nightmare. And the irony is that even when you tell a hundred students not to do it, and explain a better approach to setting out their exam answers, 5 per cent will ignore your recommendations and still do it. Do not be one of these people. Take a hint. Looking at a full page of text with no obvious paragraphs is horrible. As an examiner, instantly you think: How will I know when this person finishes dicussing one idea in the essay and moves on to the next? How will I understand how the argument in their essay develops? That is easy, you say. You will read the entire essay. Well, I challenge you. You write out a page of text with no breaks, very little space in the margins, and with no paragraphs, just line after line. Then read it 199 times over. Are you feeling refreshed and alert and ready to comprehend the arguments in the paper the 200th time you pick it up? Because that is what your examiner is facing. They might have marked 200 exams before they finally have your examination paper in their hands. At this point, you want to make your exam stand out. You want to make it easy for me to understand what you have written, and you want to make it especially easy for me to give you marks. Use space to your advantage. Like the suggestion above regarding sub-headings to distinguish when you are discussing a new idea in the essay. Use a single line space between paragraphs. Write a paragraph of text–six or seven sentences line after line like this. Then when it comes time to end your paragraph, skip a line on the examination book before you start your next paragraph. Looking at the two examples on this page, you can instantly see the difference created. Without knowing what the person has written, you are alert to the fact that they have several points to their argument and as a marker you are looking forward to seeing how they develop each point. Faced with the thought of reading Option A on the page, you are reminded about that headache that was coming on.

Exam Essay B

Sub-headings
One of the problems any examination marker faces is how to know easily when you have changed direction in an essay, or are emphasising a new point. I recommend using sub-headings in your examination, just like those used in this book. Each time you see a sub-heading it is a clue to what the paragraph is about, and as an examiner you mentally prepare yourself knowing that the previous idea is over, and a new idea is about to commence. This is doubly important in an essay written under exam conditions. You want to make it absolutely clear when you are talking about a particular idea, and when you change topic, and begin discussing a different idea.

Sub-headings are a foolproof indicator. Also they are a helpful prompt to you also to check if you have covered all the points in the essay that you said you were going to cover. In less than a minute you can flick back through several pages of text and eye up the sub-headings. Seeing a full page of text–line after line of writing–pushed out to the margins of the page with no paragraphs anywhere in sight is an examiner's nightmare. And the irony is that even when you tell a hundred students not to do it, and explain a better approach to setting out their exam answers, 5 per cent will ignore your recommendations and still do it. Do not be one of these people.

Take a hint. Looking at a full page of text with no obvious paragraphs is horrible. As an examiner, instantly you think: How will I know when this person finishes dicussing one idea in the essay and moves on to the next? How will I understand how the argument in their essay develops? That is easy, you say. You will read the entire essay. Well, I challenge you. You write out a page of text with no breaks, very little space in the margins, and with no paragraphs, just line after line. Then read it 199 times over. Are you feeling refreshed and alert and ready to comprehend the arguments in the paper the 200th time you pick it up? Because that is what your examiner is facing. They might have marked 200 exams before they finally have your examination paper in their hands.

The Next Thing
At this point, you want to make your exam stand out. You want to make it easy for me to understand what you have written, and you want to make it especially easy for me to give you marks. Use space to your advantage. Like the suggestion above regarding sub-headings to distinguish when you are discussing a new idea in the essay. Use a single line space between paragraphs. Write a paragraph of text–six or seven sentences line after line like this.

Looking at the two examples above, you can instantly see the difference. Exam essay A is a mass of words. Who knows what ideas are buried within this stream of consciousness? Exam essay B is clear and easy to follow. Even without knowing the topic, the layout alone has alerted you to the fact that there are several paragraphs, each containing a point, and two clear sub-sections to the essay (the sub-headings). Which version are you looking forward to reading? Which version will be easier to assign marks to?

Diagrams

Students ask: Should we use diagrams in an examination? The answer is that it depends on the subject. If you believe that a diagram can help you to convey the essence of your argument in a powerful way, and will usefully illustrate some point in your essay so that the marker will understand it more clearly, then use one. But just a couple of words of caution: You are sitting an exam, not an art competition. Draw your diagram using a single-coloured pen, and freehand. In other words, take 30 seconds to draw your diagram, and then continue with your writing. You will win no marks in your essay for beautifully coloured pictures, or careful use of a ruler demonstrating your ability to draw perfectly straight lines, or a colourful border. Draw quickly, freehand, using a single colour. Then keep writing.

The List Of Do-Nots

In an exam, DO NOT do the following. They waste time and distract you from your objective:

- Do not write out the question again at the start of the essay. You do not have time.
- Do not spend time defining concepts, unless the question specifically asks you to do it.
- Do not write lengthy introductory paragraphs; get into your answer rapidly.
- Do not write lists of bullet points for an essay question: they will not earn you marks. You need to amplify and expand on your ideas.
- Do not forget to plan your time. There is nothing worse than someone writing two brilliant essays for an exam, only to run out of time one page into their third and not complete it.

Don't give definitions unless asked to do so—it's analysis that wins marks in exams.

Handwriting

I know it is hard for some people, but in an exam situation you must write clearly. If you have very messy writing, then slow down, or, if necessary, print instead of using cursive script. The person marking your essay cannot give you a mark if they cannot read your essay. Also, markers are under no obligation to spend hours attempting to decipher difficult text. If they cannot read it, they do not have to give it marks.

Effective Exam Practice

Practice is the best way to study for writing an exam essay. One of the traps some students fall into is that they think that reading is studying. It is not. It is reading. You do not have to write notes in your examination; you have to write an essay. Practise doing just that.

On the day of the exam, you don't sit down to read a book, you sit down to write an essay. Of course, get information, but make essay writing the centre of your study habit.

This is especially useful if you are someone who does not have a lot of time to prepare for your examinations. Perhaps you are working part time, perhaps illness or family difficulty has limited the time that you have to devote to your studies. Do not panic. Realise that over half of all students misspend the time that they have to study because they confuse reading with studying.

Studying is active. It is practising what you have to perform. If your exam calls for you to write three essays, then practise writing three essays—again and again. It may become boring, but what will you become good at? Writing three essays.

If you are stuck for questions to write, get the past few years' examination papers. Your school, college, or university library usually has them available. Photocopy yourself a set and go to it. Previous questions are a useful guide to style and approach. In addition, if you practise doing what you have to do on examination day you get several benefits:

1. You will familiarise yourself with the material in an active (not passive) way, engaging your mind to think about what it says and how it is best expressed. Endless reading does not give you this.

2. You will practise composing and structuring answers that your mind can recall on the day.

3. You will identify gaps in your learning. As you write your practice essays you will discover times when you run out of things to say, or need to clarify a point, or find more detail. At such times, stop and go find that information so that the next time you practise writing your essay you can fill these gaps in and complete your work to a higher standard. You will have raised your potential grade as a result.

> *Practising what you have to do on exam day is the best way to strengthen your knowledge, and identify the areas where you need to improve.*

4. You will identify if your handwriting is a problem and can take steps to rectify this.

5. You will identify whether you can even write the average number of pages expected for the essay in the required time. If you cannot, at least you have time to improve your style and practise writing at a faster pace.

6. You will sometimes discover that you have answered the very question (or close to it) that is asked in the examination. Examiners are busy people, just like you. They have favourite questions or topics, sometimes they are just overloaded, and novelty becomes difficult. They adapt or repeat questions from previous examinations. If you use this method of study, that's a bonus for you. You could well find yourself sitting in an examination room staring at a question that you have already written an essay on three or four times over.

Planning Your Time

A final point for examination essays: just as you plan your essay, plan your time in the examination. Divide the number of marks in your exam by the number of minutes you have to perform that exam. So, for example, if you were sitting a three-hour exam worth 100 marks, you have 100 marks spread over 180 minutes. That gives 1.8 minutes per mark. If each essay was worth 25 marks, then you have 45 minutes per essay.

You should allow yourself a couple of minutes at the start of each essay to plan, as well as five minutes at the end of each essay to read over what you have written and make any quick corrections or deletions. For this exam, it would give you 38 minutes of writing time per essay, which should be enough time to write three pages of text per answer.

You can use this formula whatever combination of essay/examination time you have to prepare for. The important point is that once you work out the time allocations for your examination, you stick to them in the exam.

If you run out of time toward the end of an essay, leave some space, then go on to the next essay question. If you have time at the end of the examination, go back and finish the question that you could not complete earlier.

Plan to finish. There are no marks for good intentions.

It is more important that you complete all the questions than complete, for example, three out of four brilliantly, and run out of time completely to tackle the final essay.

For example, you obtain higher overall marks from writing four essays of B+ standard in your examination, than you do from writing two essays of A+ standard, an A- essay, and nothing for the final essay—because you ran out of time. That scenario would only give you an overall score of B- at best, and more likely a C+. In short, completion is vital if you are going to score the most marks you can in your examination—and completion is all about planning and practice.

CHAPTER NINE

Polishing Your Work

Some people find it easy to get their thoughts down on paper. But, as you will have realised, this is only the first step. You need to apply polish—especially if you want to have a chance at higher grades. The difference between an A and an A+ can be slight. It is often revealed in extra shine that a student was able to apply to an essay. One student may have used exactly the same information and argued exactly the same perspective on a topic as someone else, but the way they delivered their thoughts just had that something extra. In this chapter we explore how to achieve just that.

Writing Is Not A Flash Of Brilliance

The first myth that we need to dispel is that great essays are written in a single draft. It is simply not true. People who write for a living are not so incredibly brilliant that the perfect word spills off their pen the moment it hits the page, like oil gushing from a newly tapped well. That view of writing is fantasy, not reality. The process to produce clear, lucid, interesting writing involves drafting and redrafting.

If you are committed to improving your work (and I hope you are), I want you to begin thinking of your essay-writing process as three drafts. Not three entirely new drafts. That is not necessary. But three drafts to get your essay to the point where it is of a higher standard than you have previously attained.

Draft One

The first draft is your initial effort to get all the words of your essay down on paper. You have planned it out according to the suggestions in this book, assembled your evidence, and written your essay. This will not have occurred in one sitting, but over several days you will have your first attempt finished. Some of you have handed in your work at this point: don't. You are only at stage one in the drafting process and the very best you can do is still to emerge. So wait and move to draft number two.

Draft Two

At this point you draft for content. As you go through your work, ask yourself several questions:

- Have I substantiated all my points?
- Have I eliminated generalisations?
- Have I got only one idea per paragraph?
- Are my points well developed and clearly thought through?
- Are the paragraphs in the best order to clearly put across the subject and the idea? Would a different order produce a stronger argument or one that was easier to understand?
- Is there more information that I need in order to better state a point, or make something clearer to the reader?

Draft two is about being tough with yourself. You must develop the capacity to critique your work. If initially you find this difficult, take it to a friend, teacher, or tutor and ask them to look over the essay and tell you where you could make some improvements.

Tell them that your essay is still in the drafting stage but that you would value their comments. Listen and note down what they say. Hold back the urge to interrupt after each of their suggestions and defend why you have or haven't done something. When you come away from the discussion, ask yourself:

- Did they make comments like: 'I'm not sure I understand what you are saying here'?, 'I think you need to make this clearer'?
- Did they say something like: 'That's interesting; I would like to

know more about that'?

These are all clues that you have more work to do and that the best essay you can write is still to emerge. Accept this sort of feedback graciously. This person is saving you from error and helping you to get higher grades.

Draft Three

After you have made the sorts of improvements that draft two called for, you begin draft three. This is drafting for detail. Here you look for the following:

- Look for typographical errors and spelling mistakes.
- Check your grammar.
- Do you have too many of the same style of sentence in a paragraph, or words or phrases repeated too often and too close together?
- Check that you have been consistent with your word usage: for example, don't write thing like 'First World War' in one place in your essay and 'WWI' in another. Do the same throughout.
- Are all your references included in your reference list or bibliography? Have you put them in the correct style and format?
- Have you given your essay a title?
- Have you written your name on your work? You would be surprised how many people forget to do so.

It is this sort of polish that takes an essay up a grade point. If the marker has two essays in front of them, with identical content and arguing the same points, and one has unnecessary typographical errors, or clumsy spelling mistakes, or missed references, or has repeated words or phrases, this one will often score a grade less than the polished essay. The polished essay says that the person writing it has taken the time to make it their best. They have paid attention to not only the grand themes but also the little details, which if missed, detract from what was being attempted.

Removing Clever Work

When you are in draft three of the editing process I want to suggest a challenge. One of the barriers to great writing is cleverness. It happens to all of us. You are busy working away on a piece of work, when a brilliant turn of phrase crosses your mind, and you write it down. You smile to yourself, proud of your new-found literary ability. But you have just committed the sin of cleverness. Or, if I was to now commit this mistake myself: your grandiloquent expression has got in the way of stupendous writing.

Typically, when we think we have been really clever with our expressions, or descriptions, or sentence structures, we have written in a way that is hard for the reader to understand. We have put a stumbling block in the way of clarity and readability.

The solution is to eliminate these passages. Go back through your work and cross out the places where you think your writing or turn of phrase has been really clever or smart. Rewrite them in a plainer, more straightforward way. I am not suggesting that you write in a way that is elementary. But pick the right word, and one that makes it easy for the reader to understand what you are saying.

Remember: the goal of good academic writing is clarity. You are communicating your argument on a topic. If someone has to read each of your sentences twice to comprehend what you are saying because you have used complex phrasing, or pretentious words, then you have failed the clarity test. You have written something, but you have not communicated it as powerfully or as well as you might have. Remove some of the stumbling blocks for the reader. Go back through your work and eliminate the places where you are far too proud of your literary skill.

Distance And Time

All these editing suggestions will be a lot easier to undertake if you master the advantages that time and distance have to offer. Rushing to complete your essay the night before it is due might get it done, but you lose the opportunity to employ a vital ally in the writing process—time.

I am sure you will have experienced at some point writing something once and thinking you did a really good job of it, then some days later going back to the piece you have written and re-reading it, only to realise that it wasn't very good at all. This does not mean that you are a bad

> Use time to your advantage. Taking a break between drafts will give your brain some of the space it needs to see new connections in your work.

writer—actually, just the reverse. You are harnessing the advantages that time has to offer.

Putting distance between yourself and your work gives you the opportunity to make fresh judgements and gain better perspective. When you are deeply immersed in your work your capacity to act like this is clouded. Our minds are so full with the immediate details and thoughts on the page in front of us that we cannot stand back and read something objectively, or with a critical eye.

To achieve this I recommend the two-day rule. Take the essay draft you are working on, place it in your desk drawer and come back to it two days later. You will get several benefits from this. Firstly, you will come back to it with fresh eyes, and so when you read it again it will appear new and your mind will be in a better state to make judgements about how good, or not, sections of your essay are. Listen to what your head tells you at this point—it is important.

Secondly, putting some time between you and the work will have allowed your brain to think over the words that you put down on paper and the arguments that you are making. New connections and insights will come to you during this interlude. You will realise additional points that you might cover, or how you might deal with information in a better and clearer way. These are benefits that time and distance gives. You cannot manufacture this any other way. And, as a writer, it is a major aid to producing better work.

You do not want your marker to be the first person who reads your essay and sees all those things that you thought were brilliant, but several days later, show they needed further development. Plan ahead—use the benefits that distance and time can bring to your work.

Listen To Improve

Sentences have rhythm. Syllables, phrases, pauses, punctuation—all work together to produce the natural flow and tempo of a sentence. Create a difficult rhythm, and the reader has to constantly stop and re-read what you have said to understand the point that you are trying to make. Create an ease to your expression, and the marker will effortlessly move through your work: how you express yourself assists what you are trying to say.

So think about rhythm. The best way to get a sense of this is to read your work aloud. Pick a quiet spot and read your essay out loud to yourself. Not only will you sense if the natural rhythm of your sentences works, you will also get other benefits:

- You will quickly recognise whether your ideas connect one to the other.
- You will hear whether you have supported your points with logical and sound evidence.
- You will sense whether you have used too many sentences of the same style or type.
- You will discover missing words or grammatical errors. (It is easy to miss these in silent reading.)

So read out loud. It is a route to polishing your essay and improving what you have written.

The Trap Of Overwriting

Finally, one of the dangers in academic writing is overwriting. Even good essays are guilty of this habit. Instead of saying something clearly and simply, they play it out, and all of a sudden what could be said powerfully and insightfully in a couple of sentences fills half a page. It is overwriting. There is far too much padding and unnecessary information. The writer uses two sentences to say the same thing, when one sentence would do. I have just done it now without even realising it. So watch out; it is an easy mistake to make.

There are three main causes of overwriting in academic essays. The first is lack of editing. Using the three-draft process outlined earlier in this chapter should eliminate this problem. Carefully, you will put aside time to read through your essay looking for and eliminating unnecessary repetition.

The second cause of overwriting is inserting too many examples into a paragraph to make a point. Sometimes, a person will support a point with a good, detailed example, then right when you think you should be at the end of the paragraph, off they go again—out comes another lengthy example, possibly even a third. Don't do it. Keep your writing tight. You are not going to get three times the mark for reciting multiple, long examples on the same phenomenon. Write another paragraph and deliver fresh insight.

The third cause is lack of reading on the topic. Most people who make the mistake of overwriting are not bad writers; they are good writers, but they have not read enough material on their question topic. When they come to write their essays, they run out of things to say and unconsciously stretch what they do know to unwieldy lengths. The result is an essay that says too little in far too many words.

What's the solution? Read more widely. Read so you have plenty of interesting things to say. Read so you can be insightful, clear, and engaging in your essay. Ironically, you will not waste time by doing this, you will gain time. You will speed up the writing phase of your essay because you will not find yourself sitting there wondering what on earth you are going to say next. You will have plenty of words to write.

Conclusion

Enough time spent reading: now is the moment to let your talent shine!

We have traversed a lot of ground together in this book. We have covered planning, writing, sentence styles, essay structure, how to say what you want to say, crafting your arguments, referencing, how to write essays in exam conditions, how to polish your work, and many other topics.

I would like to conclude this book with an encouragement. Recently, I spent some time with one of my students going over his essay. He had made a fair effort, but it was not as good as it could have been—nor did it reflect his true ability. I knew he was capable of much more: he understood the research he was reading, and even enjoyed the subject, but he had not yet learned how to convey his ideas on paper in the most convincing or powerful way.

We sat down and began talking about essay writing. We talked about the introduction to the essay, and what it needed to say; about the importance of making your argument clear and explicit from the outset. We discussed making the point of each paragraph clear in the first sentence and using different forms of evidence to support points in a convincing way. We changed some of his sentences, so that they were not all the same repetitive style, and he quickly realised how he could communicate what he wanted to say much more effectively. I explained how to weigh evidence—like a courtroom lawyer—exposing weaknesses and discussing merits. Finally, we talked about polishing his work—ordering his ideas in the best possible way, eliminating repetition, and checking for grammar.

At the end of ten minutes his whole face lit up. 'Nobody has ever told me this,' he declared.

'Well,' I replied, 'now you know. Why don't you bring me a revised version in a week's time and we'll discuss it further. I'm sure it's going to be a big improvement on this.'

'It sure will be!' he agreed, as he bundled his papers together and left. His new-found confidence was obvious.

A week later, he proudly showed me what he had written. Right from the first sentence, it was obvious that this second version of his essay was far better than the first. And all his essays will be better from now on— because he knows what is expected of him and he has a range of tools at his disposal to make the changes that he needs to make. He has started to develop the skills of academic essay writing.

You have even greater advantages. Because, unlike him, you have an entire book on this subject and have just learned things that I could never tell him about in the brief time we spent together. If you consciously put into practice what you have read in these pages you will write better essays, and you will score higher grades than you did before. You will know how to avoid the common mistakes that your fellow students make; you will display greater depth and control over your writing; you will be able to express yourself and your arguments in ways that you could not previously and with fresh clarity—and you will probably even start to enjoy writing essays!

Just remember that as a writer and a thinker, you already have many fine skills and abilities. To get to where you are today, you have probably spent a significant portion of your life in study and learning. The difference this book will make is that the next time you pick up your pen, the talent which you already possess will start to shine in an entirely new way. Now, write that essay!

All the best,

Dr Ian Hunter
Auckland, 2012